Discovering

Advanced

Algebra
An Investigative
Approach

Assessment Resources B

DISCOVERING

MATHEMATICS

Key Curriculum Press
Innovators in Mathematics Education

Teacher's Materials Project Editor: Joan Lewis

Project Editor: Heather Dever

Editor: Stacey Miceli

Editorial Assistants: Erin Gray, Eric Martin

Writers: Jerald Murdock, Josephine Noah, David Rasmussen, Karen Wootten

Accuracy Checker: Dudley Brooks

Production Editor: Angela Chen

Copyeditor: Janet Greenblatt

Editorial Production Manager: Deborah Cogan

Production Director: Diana Jean Ray

Production Coordinator: Ann Rothenbuhler

Text Designer: Jenny Somerville

Art Editor: Jason Luz

Composition, Technical Art: Interactive Composition Corporation

Art and Design Coordinator: Marilyn Perry

Cover Designer: Jill Kongabel

Printer: Von Hoffmann Corporation

Executive Editor: Casey FitzSimons

Publisher: Steven Rasmussen

Cover Photo Credits: Background and center images: NASA;
all other images: Ken Karp Photography.

Key Curriculum Press
1150 65th Street
Emeryville, CA 94608
(510) 595-7000
editorial@keypress.com
www.keypress.com

Printed in the United States of America
10 9 8 7 6 5 4 3 2   07 06 05   ISBN 1-55953-611-X

Contents

Chapter 6

Chapters 4–6 Exam

Chapter 7

Chapter 8

Chapter 9

Chapters 7–9 Exam

Chapter 10

Chapter 11

Introduction

Assessment Resources B includes quizzes, chapter tests, cumulative exams, and constructive assessments, answers, and rubrics for use with *Discovering Advanced Algebra: An Investigative Approach.* These written assessments are not the only way for you to evaluate your students, but they are one way to let you and your students know what they have learned.

Quizzes and Tests

This volume includes one test and as many as three quizzes for each chapter. Each quiz covers material from two or three lessons, and the test covers material from the entire chapter. Four cumulative exams are also provided, covering Chapters 1–3, Chapters 4–6, Chapters 7–9, and Chapters 10–13. A final exam covers Chapters 1–13. Alternative forms of the quizzes and tests are provided in *Assessment Resources A.*

The quizzes and tests are written assignments that pose specific, often closed-ended problems and questions designed to test a student's mastery of particular subject matter and skills. Typically, students work on quizzes and tests individually and are expected to complete them during a limited amount of class time.

The advantage of a traditional quiz or test is that it provides a simple tool for rating a student's understanding of the material. You can usually translate a test result into a numerical grade fairly easily. This gives you, students, and parents objective feedback on how well the students are doing.

Traditional timed tests are stressful for many students. Some students suffer from so much test anxiety that they simply cannot complete their tests. (Of course, there are also those students who perform at their best in these situations.) Here are some ideas for making traditional testing less stressful. One strategy is to allow students to create and bring a collection of notes on a notecard or sheet of paper that they can refer to during a test. Teachers find that students do some useful review as they put their notes together. Discourage students from sharing notecards and guard against opportunities for copying information from students who took the same test earlier, perhaps by collecting cards at the end of the test day. Also, you might want to require that each notecard be in the student's own handwriting so that students don't borrow or duplicate those of other students. Some teachers collect the notecards and count them as part of the test grade. Students often find that they hardly ever look at their notecards during the test, but they feel less pressure by having it handy.

Some teachers allow students to use their notebooks during tests and quizzes. This encourages students to keep their notebooks organized. Sometimes teachers even allow students to use their books. This encourages them to read and learn to navigate through their mathematics book. Remind students that good problem solving involves knowing how to use the proper resources.

You can also alleviate test anxiety by allowing students to retake tests. The disadvantage to this strategy is that it requires extra time for you to make and correct a second set of tests. Some teachers require students to correct their first test completely before they are allowed a retake. Some teachers permit students to keep the highest grade from the two tests, but many prefer to average the grades or require that the second grade count as the only grade. (This last technique cuts down on the number of students who opt for the retake test.)

It is not always a good idea to test students on how quickly they can work mathematics problems. Good mathematical reasoning is a systematic and thoughtful process. For this reason, it is fair to allow students extra time to finish a test if they need it. This is especially accommodating for students who may have linguistic, physical, emotional, or psychological needs that slow them down. It can be hard to find the extra time to allow students to finish. Sometimes it is worth having students come in after school or at lunchtime to allow them the few extra minutes they need. Be alert to students who misuse this privilege and discuss test questions outside class before they return to finish.

Constructive Assessment Options

This volume also includes constructive assessment items for each chapter. These items are deeper and richer than items on the tests and quizzes. While the quiz and test items tend to call for definitive answers, most constructive assessment items are open-ended, with many possible correct answers. And, while quiz and test items assess particular skills, constructive assessment items assess a student's ability to explain, apply, connect, and extend the important concepts of the lessons.

Here are some suggestions for how you might use these items.

- Use three or four constructive assessment items in place of a traditional chapter test.
- Create a chapter test by combining one or two constructive assessment items with items from the chapter test.
- Include one constructive assessment item as an extra-credit problem on the chapter test.
- Use the constructive assessment items on take-home tests.
- Assign the items as additional homework questions for extra credit.

Because of their open-ended nature, constructive assessment items can be more difficult to score than traditional test items. The answer section of this book provides a rubric for each item, giving criteria for 5-point, 3-point, and 1-point answers. See *Assessment Resources A* for examples of how to use the rubrics.

Creating Individual Assessment

Items from both forms of the tests and constructive assessments are available electronically on the *Test Generator and Worksheet Builder*™ CD. These items can be part of any test you create with the test generator. Using the *Worksheet Builder*™ software, you can combine items from this book with any of the dozens of other items for each chapter.

If you do not want to change the chapter tests, copy them from this book or print them directly from the *Test Generator* CD, where they exist as saved worksheets. The constructive assessment items for each chapter are also on the test generator as saved worksheets, but those saved worksheets should not be printed out as tests because each contains many more items than would be reasonable for a timed test. These harder items have been included as saved worksheets only so that the items (and their scoring rubrics) would be available for tests you create, which could have one or two constructive assessment items and a few shorter questions. Instructions for using the test generator are on the *Test Generator* CD and in the *Quick Start Guide* included with the CD.

Other Opportunities for Assessment

These materials are only some of the assessment opportunities available. Because *Discovering Algebra* engages students as active learners, it provides ample opportunities to assess student learning throughout the course. Investigations and Explorations provide opportunities for performance assessment (assessment that focuses on the student's thought process). Exercises and other features can stimulate portfolio entries and presentations. Projects in the student book give students opportunities to demonstrate their learning in new contexts. Each chapter ends with Assessing What You've Learned, a chance for students to write in their journals, organize their notebooks, update their portfolios, give a presentation, or do a performance assessment.

It is always best to mix traditional testing with other types of assessment. A good mix helps accommodate the various learning styles and needs of your students, and it allows you to show that there are many different ways of doing and learning mathematics.

Chapter 0 • Test

Name _____ Period _____ Date _____

Answer each question and show all work clearly on a separate piece of paper.

1. A line passes through the point $(5, -7)$ and has slope $-\frac{4}{5}$. Find another point on the same line.

2. Jason needs to measure exactly 5 liters of water. He has only two containers—one that holds exactly 4 liters and one that holds exactly 7 liters. Describe or illustrate a procedure that will give exactly 5 liters of water in one of the containers.

3. Jing received a paycheck from her part-time job. She spent some of the money getting her car fixed and some on dinner and a concert. She deposited the rest in her savings account. The total amount she spent was $159. The amount she saved was 25% more than the amount she spent on dinner and a concert. The amount she spent on her car was $15 more than the amount she saved. What was the total amount of Jing's paycheck?

4. Tom, Harry, and Bob are brothers. Use these clues to determine the sport each boy plays, his favorite school subject, and whether he is the youngest, middle, or oldest.

   • The brother who plays tennis is either the oldest or the youngest.

   • Harry plays football.

   • The brother who likes music best is *not* the closest in age to Bob.

   • The brother on the track team is older than the brother who likes science.

   • Harry, the brother on the tennis team, and the brother who likes Latin are three different people.

   • Tom is not on the track team.

5. Expand each product.

   a. $(x + 7)(x - 7)$ **b.** $(5 + z)(y - 12)$ **c.** $(m - p)^2$

6. Find the slope of the line that passes through each pair of points.

   a. $(2, 0), (3, 7)$ **b.** $(-4, 2), (1, 6)$ **c.** $(-3, 7), (3, 1)$

7. Use the Pythagorean Theorem to find each missing length.

   a. 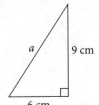   **b.**   **c.**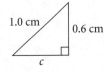

(continued)

8. Substitute the given value of the variable(s) in each expression and evaluate.

   a. $12 + x^2$ when $x = -3$

   b. $\dfrac{32 - 5p}{2q}$ when $p = 4$ and $q = 2$

   c. 4^x when $x = 4$

9. Use the properties of exponents to rewrite each expression so that the variable appears only once.

   a. $(z^5)(z)$　　　　b. $\dfrac{t^5}{t^8}$　　　　c. $3(2y^3)^5$　　　　d. $\dfrac{(x^7)(x^3)}{x^9}$

10. Solve each equation.

    a. $-3(x - 7) + 10 = 40$

    b. $5x = -2 - (x - 6)$

    c. $(x - 5)(3x + 9) = 0$

11. Translate each verbal statement into a symbolic expression.

    a. Five less than nine times a number

    b. Ten more than the square of a number

    c. Seven divided by the sum of a number and one

12. Jodie rode her bike 22 miles in 2 hours. What was her average riding speed in feet per second? Give your answer to the nearest tenth.

Chapter 0 • Constructive Assessment Options

Choose one or more of these items to replace part of the chapter test. Let students know that they will receive from 0 to 5 points for each item, depending on the correctness and completeness of their answer.

1. *(Lessons 0.1–0.3)*

Albert and Bob are on a hiking trip. Each is carrying a pack. If Albert were to take enough of Bob's stuff to increase the weight of his own pack by a third, he would have half of the combined weight inside both packs. If Bob were to take 3 pounds of Albert's stuff, he'd have three-quarters of the combined weight. How much weight is each man carrying? Show and explain each step of your solution.

2. *(Lessons 0.1–0.3)*

Jermain's round pizzas are famous for their spicy crust. Jermain cuts his pizzas with four strokes of his knife, always going completely across from outer crust to outer crust.

a. If Jermain cuts his pizza the usual way, with each stroke of the knife passing through the center of the pizza, how many pieces will be created? How many pieces will have crust?

b. In how many different ways can Jermain slice a pizza with four cuts? Consider two pizzas to be sliced differently if they have a different number of pieces *or* a different number of pieces with crust. The size of the pieces does not matter. Show and label all the possibilities.

Chapter 1 • Quiz 1

Name _____ Period _____ Date _____

In Problems 1 and 2, tell whether the sequence generated by the recursive formula is arithmetic or geometric. Then write the first four terms of the sequence.

1. $u_1 = 12$
$u_n = \frac{1}{4} \cdot u_{n-1}$ where $n \geq 2$

2. $u_1 = 11$
$u_n = u_{n-1} - 7$ where $n \geq 2$

In Problems 3 and 4, write a recursive formula that generates each sequence, and then find the given term. (Use u_1 to represent the starting term.)

3. 1, -2, 4, -8, 16 . . .   Find the 10th term.

4. 20, 17.5, 15, 12.5, 10 . . . Find the 12th term.

5. A bouncing ball is modeled by the recursive formula $u_0 = 120$ and $u_n = (1 - 0.25)u_{n-1}$ where $n \geq 1$. Give real-world meanings for the numbers 120 and 0.25.

6. Alma has just received job offers from both ACME, Inc. and Widget.com. Both companies have offered her a salary of $40,000 for the first year. ACME, Inc. tells Alma they will increase her salary by 5% each year. Widget.com says they will increase her salary by $2500 each year.

a. For each company, write a recursive formula for calculating Alma's salary in the nth year.

b. Complete the table.

Salary		
Year	ACME, Inc.	Widget.com
1	$40,000	$40,000
2		
3		
4		
5		

c. Alma decides to accept the job with ACME, Inc. When will her salary at ACME first surpass the salary she would have been making at Widget.com?

Chapter 1 • Quiz 2

Name _____ Period _____ Date _____

1. At the beginning of January, the Bike MegaMart has 400 bicycles in stock. Each month they plan to sell 20% of their stock. On the last day of each month, they will receive a shipment of 120 new bikes.

   a. Write a recursive formula for calculating the number of bikes in stock at the end of n months.

   b. How many bikes will the MegaMart have at the end of 12 months?

   c. Describe what will happen to the number of bikes in stock over the long run.

In Problems 2–4, imagine the graph of the sequence generated by the recursive formula. Describe the graph using exactly three of these terms: arithmetic, decreasing, geometric, increasing, linear, nonlinear, shifted geometric.

2. $u_0 = 10$
   $u_n = 0.78 \cdot u_{n-1}$ where $n \geq 1$

3. $u_0 = 0$
   $u_n = 0.4 \cdot u_{n-1} + 50$ where $n \geq 1$

4. $u_0 = 75$
   $u_n = u_{n-1} + 25$ where $n \geq 1$

5. Dante deposited $10,000 into an account with an annual interest rate of 3.75%, compounded quarterly. He plans to deposit an additional $750 each quarter, just after the interest is compounded. What will his balance be after five years?

Discovering Advanced Algebra Assessment Resources B
©2004 Key Curriculum Press

Chapter 1 • Test

Name _____ Period _____ Date _____

Answer each question and show all work clearly on a separate piece of paper.

1. Here are the first three figures of a pattern.

   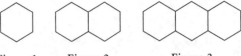

   Figure 1   Figure 2   Figure 3

   a. List the numbers of line segments in Figures 1–7.

   b. Write a recursive formula that generates the sequence you found in part a.

   c. How many line segments are in Figure 21?

   d. Which figure has 211 line segments?

2. Consider the sequence 0.01, 0.03, 0.09, 0.27, 0.81, ...

   a. Is the sequence arithmetic or geometric? Justify your answer.

   b. Write a recursive formula for the sequence. Use u_1 to represent the starting term.

   c. What is the 9th term of the sequence?

   d. Which term of the sequence is the first to be greater than 10,000?

3. Suppose $80,000 is invested in an account that pays 7.25% annual interest, compounded monthly.

   a. If no money is deposited or withdrawn, what will the balance be after 10 years?

   b. If $150 is added to the account every month just after the interest is compounded, what will the balance be after 10 years?

4. A mortgage of $100,000 is to be paid off in exactly 30 years. If the annual interest rate is 6.75%, compounded monthly, what will the monthly payment be?

5. A small country has a population of 2.5 million people. Each year about 4% of the previous year's population dies or leaves the country and about 120,000 people are born or immigrate to the country. If this pattern continues, what will the population be in 5 years? What will the population be in the long run?

6. Give the recursive formula for a sequence whose graph fits the given description.

   a. Nonlinear and decreasing

   b. Linear and increasing

   c. Nonlinear and increasing, with a long-run value that is not zero

Chapter 1 • Constructive Assessment Options

Choose one or more of these items to replace part of the chapter test. Let students know that they will receive from 0 to 5 points for each item, depending on the correctness and completeness of their answer.

1. *(Lessons 1.1, 1.3)*

Consider the shifted geometric sequence generated by this rule:

$$u_1 = 4$$
$$u_n = 3u_{n-1} + 4 \quad \text{where } n \geq 2$$

a. List the first six terms of the sequence.

b. List the differences of consecutive terms for the sequence you found in part a.

c. Look at the sequence of consecutive differences you found in part b. What kind of sequence is it? What is its recursive formula? How does this formula compare with the formula for the original shifted geometric sequence?

d. The sequence 1640, 408, 100, 23, $\frac{15}{4}$, $-\frac{17}{16}$, . . . is a shifted geometric sequence. Use the observations you made in parts b and c to help you find the recursive formula that generates this sequence. Explain your procedure.

2. *(Lessons 1.1, 1.2)*

Suppose you are given a choice about how you will be paid for a job that gets harder and harder each week. For both plans, you receive $50 the first week. Under plan A, you get a $5 raise each week. Under plan B, you receive a 5% increase each week.

a. For each plan, write a recursive formula you could use to calculate your pay.

b. Make a chart comparing the pay under each plan for weeks 5, 10, 15, 20, and 25. Show the amounts the two plans pay and the difference in the amounts.

c. Which plan pays a higher weekly salary for the first several weeks? When does the salary from the other plan become greater?

d. Discuss the issues you would consider when deciding which plan to take.

(continued)

Discovering Advanced Algebra Assessment Resources B
©2004 Key Curriculum Press

3. *(Lesson 1.3)*

An ordinary car depreciates each year, so that eventually it isn't worth much of anything. A luxury car that is well maintained, however, depreciates less and less each year and in the long run maintains a certain value. The following rule might be used to model the value of a luxury car, originally valued at $93,995, over time:

$$u_0 = 93995$$
$$u_n = (1 - 0.2)u_{n-1} + 6000 \quad \text{where } n \geq 1$$

a. What is the value of the car after one year? After nine years? After ten years?

b. What is the percent of depreciation for the first year? From the ninth to the tenth year? Give your answers to the nearest tenth of a percent. Show the calculations you used to find the answers.

c. After how many years will the value of the car drop below $32,000?

d. Use the recursive rule to find the long-run value of the car. Explain your procedure.

e. Sketch a graph showing the car's value over 25 years.

Chapter 2 • Quiz 1

Name _____ Period _____ Date _____

1. Invent a data set with eight values that has a mean of 15 and a median of 17.

2. The data below show the number of homework problems Mr. Rivera and Ms. Jensen assigned to their algebra classes each night for the last two weeks.

    Mr. Rivera: 9, 17, 10, 13, 12, 11, 15, 10, 14, 11

    Ms. Jensen: 5, 10, 7, 12, 0, 20, 15, 20, 8, 2

    a. Find the five-number summary for each class.

    b. Make a box plot for each set of data. Put the plots on the same axis.

    c. Use the information in the box plots to write at least three statements comparing the data for Mr. Rivera's class with the data for Ms. Jensen's class.

3. Find the standard deviation for each data set in Problem 2. What do the standard deviations indicate about how the two data sets compare?

Chapter 2 • Quiz 2

Name _____ Period _____ Date _____

This histogram shows the price (in cents) of a small box of popcorn at all the movie theaters within a 10-mile radius of a major city.

Small Popcorn Prices

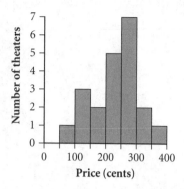

1. How many theaters are represented in the histogram?

2. What is the bin width?

3. What percent of the theaters charge $3.00 or more for a small box of popcorn?

4. A small box of popcorn at the Ritz Theater costs $1.50. What is the percentile rank of the Ritz?

5. Estimate the median price. Explain how you made your estimate.

Discovering Advanced Algebra Assessment Resources B
©2004 Key Curriculum Press

Chapter 2 • Test

Name_____   Period_____   Date_____

Answer each question and show all work clearly on a separate piece of paper.

In Problems 1 and 2, refer to these box plots.

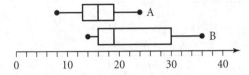

1. Describe the similarities and differences between the data sets represented by the two box plots. Your answer should include at least three comparisons.

2. Plot A represents 20 values, while plot B represents 25 values. For each plot, draw a histogram that might represent the same data.

3. Find the mean, median, mode, and standard deviation of the data below. Which two of these measures do you think best characterize the data? Explain.

   73 81 94 95 73 75 250 85 77 73 82 90 88 76 80 79

4. Create a data set with at least nine values that has a median less than 20 and a mean greater than 25. Verify that your data set satisfies these conditions.

5. Choose either histogram A or histogram B. Describe a situation or experiment that might give data with the shape shown in the histogram. Explain why the data would have the given shape.

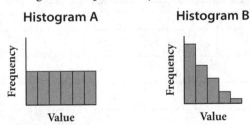

6. The table on next page lists the 2001 films that earned the most money in U.S. theaters.

(continued)

Name _____ Period _____ Date _____

Top-Grossing Films of 2001

Rank	Title	Total Domestic Gross ($ millions)
1	Harry Potter and the Sorcerer's Stone	318
2	The Lord of the Rings: The Fellowship of the Ring	313
3	Shrek	268
4	Monster's, Inc.	255
5	Rush Hour 2	226
6	The Mummy Returns	202
7	Pearl Harbor	198
8	Ocean's Eleven	183
9	Jurassic Park III	181
10	Planet of the Apes	180
11	A Beautiful Mind	171
12	Hannibal	165
13	American Pie II	145
14	The Fast and the Furious	145
15	Lara Croft: Tomb Raider	131
16	Dr. Dolittle 2	113
17	Spy Kids	113
18	Black Hawk Down	109
19	The Princess Diaries	108
20	Vanilla Sky	101

(www.the-movie-times.com)

a. Find the mean and the standard deviation of the data.

b. Give the five-number summary for the data.

c. How many movies in the table have domestic grosses within two standard deviations of the mean?

d. What is the percentile rank of *Shrek?*

e. Decide which type of graph, a histogram or a box plot, will best represent the data. Graph the data and justify your choice.

f. Write a short (5 to 10 sentences) news article about the money earned by the top-grossing movies of 2001. Include measures of central tendency and measures of spread.

Chapter 2 • Constructive Assessment Options

Choose one or more of these items to replace part of the chapter test. Let students know that they will receive from 0 to 5 points for each item, depending on the correctness and completeness of their answer.

1. *(Lesson 2.1)*
   Here are the shoe sizes for students in an eleventh-grade math class.

   Female: 8, 7, 4.5, 7, 6.5, 6, 7.5, 6, 5, 5.5, 7.5, 8, 9, 7, 7, 5.5, 6

   Male: 9, 8, 10.5, 8, 7.5, 10, 10, 10, 7, 10.5, 9, 9.5, 10, 11.5, 10.5, 12

   a. Find the mean, median, and mode shoe sizes for the females and for the males.

   b. For each group, tell which shoe size you think is most typical. Justify your answers.

   c. For each group, create a box plot of the shoe sizes. Put both plots on the same axis. Give the five-number summary for each group. Use the box plot and the statistics you calculated to help you write at least four statements comparing the shoe sizes for the two groups.

2. *(Lessons 2.2, 2.3)*
   A survey of gas stations in the San Francisco area during the last week of March 2002 found these prices (in cents) for a gallon of regular self-serve gasoline.

   139.9, 141.9, 143.9, 149.9, 149.9, 149.9, 151.9, 155.9, 155.9, 159.9, 159.9, 159.9, 159.9, 165.9, 165.9, 169.9, 175.9, 179.9, 179.9, 183.9

   a. Create a histogram of the data using 5-cent bin widths.

   b. Find the mean, median, and mode.

   c. What is the range of the prices?

   d. In March 2002, the Department of Consumer Affairs reported that the price of gas had gone up an average of 25 cents over the previous three months. Describe how a histogram for the beginning of 2002 would compare with the March histogram.

   e. Based on the information from the histogram, do you think it is worth looking for a bargain on gasoline? Justify your answer.

(continued)

3. *(Lessons 2.1, 2.2)*

Here are the heights, in feet and inches, of the players on the 2002 Boston Celtics, Detroit Pistons, and Chicago Bulls basketball teams.

Celtics: 6-1, 6-11, 7-0, 6-7, 6-2, 6-4, 6-10, 6-8, 6-6, 6-10, 6-7, 6-3, 6-9, 6-8

Pistons: 6-10, 5-11, 5-11, 6-5, 6-8, 6-5, 6-3, 7-0, 7-0, 6-10, 6-6, 7-1, 6-9, 6-9, 6-7

Bulls: 7-1, 5-11, 7-1, 6-5, 6-11, 6-9, 6-1, 6-5, 6-5, 6-9, 6-5, 6-9, 6-8
(*www.nba.com*)

a. Convert the heights to inches, and display the data for each team in a box plot. Put all three box plots on the same axis.

b. Give the five-number summary for each team.

c. Find the mean height for each team. How do the means compare?

d. Find the standard deviation of the heights for each team.

e. Use the box plots and the statistics you calculated to make at least five statements comparing the heights for the three teams.

4. *(Lesson 2.3)*

A prestigious math exam was administered to a large number of high school students who volunteered to pit their wit and ingenuity against ten challenging problems. The following histogram shows the results.

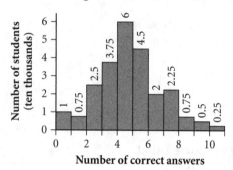

High School Math Exam

a. If a student earned 10 points for each correct answer, with no partial credit, how many students scored 70 points?

b. How many students volunteered to take the exam?

c. Mary Beth received a score of 80 points. What was her percentile ranking?

d. Simon got six correct answers. What was his percentile ranking?

e. Cheon answered every problem correctly. What was her percentile ranking? Explain what your answer means.

f. Construct two histograms showing the results of 100,000 students on a four-question test. For the data in the first histogram, a perfect score should yield a 50th-percentile ranking. For the data in the second histogram, a 50% score should yield a 99th-percentile ranking.

Chapter 3 • Quiz 1

Name _____ Period _____ Date _____

1. Write the explicit formula for the sequence defined by this recursive formula:

$$u_0 = 11$$
$$u_n = u_{n-1} - 6 \quad \text{where } n \geq 1$$

2. Write an equation for the line with slope 4.25 and y-intercept -7.

3. The graph shows the median purchase price of a home in the United States each year from 1990 through 2001.

Median Home Prices

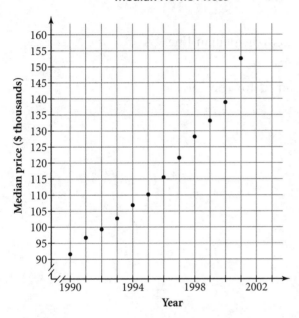

(*The World Almanac and Book of Facts 2002*)

a. Draw a line of fit that summarizes the data, and find the equation for your line.

b. Use your equation to predict the median home price in 2020.

Chapter 3 • Quiz 2

Name _____ **Period** _____ **Date** _____

In Problems 1–4, use these data.

x	7	3	10	1	4	8	2	6
y	3	8	1	10	8	6	11	5

1. Plot the points. Find the equation for the median-median line.
   Show all your work. Draw the median-median line on the same axes
   as the points.

2. Calculate the residuals and the sum of the residuals. Round the values
   to hundredths.

3. Calculate the root mean square error for the median-median line.
   Explain what the root mean square error means.

4. Do you think the median-median line is a good fit for the data?
   Give evidence to support your answer.

Discovering Advanced Algebra Assessment Resources B
©2004 Key Curriculum Press

Chapter 3 • Quiz 3

Name _____ Period _____ Date _____

1. The Alvarezes are trying to decide which of two catering companies to hire for their anniversary party. Marvelous Meals charges $700 plus $35 per person. Posh Parties charges $425 plus $50 per person. Both companies are known for their good food and excellent service, so the Alvarezes want to choose the caterer that will cost less. Which company should they hire? Explain.

In Problems 2 and 3, solve the system of equations.

2. $\begin{cases} y = 4x + 9 \\ -5x + y = 12 \end{cases}$

3. $\begin{cases} 3x + 8y = 5 \\ 5x + 4y = 27 \end{cases}$

4. Which system has no solution?

A. $\begin{cases} x + 3y = 7 \\ 3x + y = 7 \end{cases}$

B. $\begin{cases} 6x + 5y = -13 \\ y = -18x + 2 \end{cases}$

C. $\begin{cases} y = -4x + 3 \\ -16x - 4y = 12 \end{cases}$

D. $\begin{cases} -4x + 4y = 4 \\ 4x - 4y = 4 \end{cases}$

Chapter 3 • Test

Name _____ Period _____ Date _____

Answer each question and show all work clearly on a separate piece of paper.

1. Consider the arithmetic sequence defined by the formula

$$u_0 = -2.25$$
$$u_n = u_{n-1} + 1.25 \quad \text{where } n \geq 1$$

   a. Write an explicit formula for the sequence.

   b. Find the value of u_{47}.

   c. Find the value of n for which $u_n = 64$.

2. Consider the graph at right.

   a. Write the recursive formula that generates the points on the graph.

   b. Write a linear equation (in x and y) for the line that passes through the points.

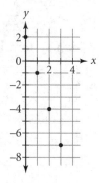

3. This graph shows the balance in Julia's checking account at the end of each month for the past year.

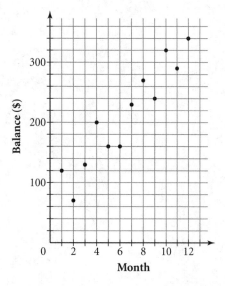

   a. Draw a line you think fits the data reasonably well.

   b. Find the equation for your line.

   c. What is the slope of your line, and what is its real-world meaning?

   d. What is the y-intercept of your line, and what is its real-world meaning?

(continued)

Discovering Advanced Algebra Assessment Resources B
©2004 Key Curriculum Press

Name_____ Period_____ Date_____

4. This table shows the average hourly earnings of U.S. production workers in years from 1970 through 2000.

Average Hourly Earnings of U.S. Production Workers

Year, x	Hourly Earnings ($), y	Year, x	Hourly Earnings ($), y
1970	3.23	1986	8.76
1972	3.70	1988	9.28
1974	4.24	1990	10.01
1976	4.86	1992	10.57
1978	5.69	1994	11.12
1980	6.66	1996	11.82
1982	7.68	1998	12.78
1984	8.32	2000	13.75

(*The World Almanac and Book of Facts 2000*)

a. Find the equation for the median-median line. (Round the slope and y-intercept to the nearest ten-thousandth.)

b. Use the median-median model to predict the average hourly earnings of production workers in 2020. Does finding this value involve interpolation or extrapolation? Explain.

c. Use the median-median model to predict the average hourly earnings of production workers in 1985. Does finding this value involve interpolation or extrapolation? Explain.

d. Calculate the residuals and the sum of the residuals for the median-median model.

e. Calculate the root mean square error for the median-median model. What is the real-world meaning of the root mean square error?

f. Based on your answers to parts d and e, do you think the median-median line is a good fit for the data? Give evidence to support your answer.

5. Solve each system of equations.

a. $\begin{cases} -6x - 7y = -34 \\ 2x + 3y = 18 \end{cases}$

b. $\begin{cases} -4x = y + 1 \\ -8x - 5y = -19 \end{cases}$

Chapter 3 • Constructive Assessment Options

Choose one or more of these items to replace part of the chapter test. Let students know that they will receive from 0 to 5 points for each item, depending on the correctness and completeness of their answer.

1. *(Lessons 3.2, 3.3)*
This table shows the life expectancy at birth for males and females in the United States during the second half of the last century.

U.S. Life Expectancy

Birth year	1950	1960	1970	1980	1990	1995	1997	1998
Male life expectancy (years)	65.6	66.6	67.1	70.0	71.8	72.5	73.6	73.8
Female life expectancy (years)	71.1	73.1	74.7	77.4	78.8	78.9	79.2	79.5

(The New York Times Almanac 2002)

a. Plot both sets of data on the same axes. Use a different symbol or color for each data set.

b. Choose two representative data points from each set, and write the equation of the line through the points.

c. Compare and interpret the slopes of the lines.

d. Use your models to predict the life expectancies for a male and a female born in 2050.

e. Do your lines intersect? If so, at what point? What is the meaning of the intersection? Does a linear model give a realistic prediction of life expectancy in 2500? Explain.

2. *(Lessons 3.3, 3.5)*
Bill and Sara conducted an experiment in which they compared the growth rates of beans under various conditions. After a bean plant broke ground, they measured its height each day for a week. One plant yielded the data shown in the table.

Bill and Sara each made a plot of the data and drew a line through two representative points to model the growth of the plant. Bill used the points $(1, 2.4)$ and $(7, 5.8)$, and Sara used $(2, 3)$ and $(5, 4.6)$.

Plant Height

Day, x	Height (cm), y
1	2.4
2	3.0
3	4.0
4	4.2
5	4.6
6	5.5
7	5.8

a. Find the equation of each model.

b. Make a table showing the day, actual height, the height values predicted by Bill's model, the height values predicted by Sara's model, and the residuals for each model.

c. Calculate the root mean square error for each model.

d. Which model is better? Justify your choice.

e. Adjust the better model to make it even better. Explain your reasoning.

(continued)

Discovering Advanced Algebra Assessment Resources B
©2004 Key Curriculum Press

3. (*Lessons 3.4, 3.5*)

This table shows the average hourly cost to industry for production workers in the United States (how much it costs a company to employ someone).

Hourly Cost to Industry of Production Workers

Year	1975	1980	1985	1990	1995	1999	2000
Cost ($)	6.36	9.87	13.01	14.91	17.91	19.11	19.86

(*The New York Times Almanac 2002*)

a. Find the median-median line for the data. Round the slope and *y*-intercept to the nearest thousandth.

b. Find the root mean square error.

c. If the trend continues, what will the cost likely be in 2010?

d. Imagine you are an industrial planner working on a seven-year expansion plan, and your company uses a large number of production workers representing a cross section of U.S. industrial workers. What range of hourly costs would you expect to have in 2010?

4. (*Lessons 3.1, 3.7*)

Sometimes two sequences intersect, sometimes they don't.

a. Find the term for which the sequences below have the same value. Give both the term number and the value of the term. Explain how you found your answer.

$$u_1 = -18$$
$$u_n = u_{n-1} + 1.4 \quad \text{where } n \geq 2$$

$$u_1 = 9$$
$$u_n = u_{n-1} + 1.1 \quad \text{where } n \geq 2$$

b. Explain why there is no term number for which the two sequences below have the same value.

$$u_1 = 6$$
$$u_n = u_{n-1} + 2.3 \quad \text{where } n \geq 2$$

$$u_1 = -30$$
$$u_n = u_{n-1} + 3 \quad \text{where } n \geq 2$$

Chapters 1–3 • Exam

Name _____ Period _____ Date _____

Answer each question and show all work clearly on a separate piece
of paper.

1. State whether each recursive formula defines a sequence that is
   arithmetic, geometric, shifted geometric, or none of these. State
   whether a graph of the sequence would be linear or curved. Then
   list the first five terms of the sequence.

   a. $u_0 = 13$
      $u_n = u_{n-1} - 9$ where $n \geq 1$

   b. $u_0 = 125$
      $u_n = (1 - 0.20)u_{n-1}$ where $n \geq 1$

2. Ted just bought a new car for $17,500. Suppose the value of the car
   decreases by 18% each year.

   a. Write a recursive formula for calculating the value of the car after
      n years.

   b. What will be the value of the car after 5 years?

   c. After how many years will the car be worth less than $5000?

3. Rashid is conducting a biology study involving fruit flies. This table
   shows the number of fruit flies in his sample at the end of each day
   for a week.

Day	1	2	3	4	5	6	7
Number of flies	40	46	54	62	72	81	94

   a. Find a recursive formula to model the population growth.

   b. Predict the number of flies in his sample at the end of 3 weeks.

   c. According to your model, when will the number of fruit flies first
      exceed 100,000?

4. Lana is recovering from surgery. She takes a pill containing 150 mg of
   pain medication every 8 hours. After 8 hours, 60% of the medicine in
   her body remains.

   a. How much medicine will be in her body 48 hours after she takes
      the first pill?

   b. How much medicine will be in her body in the long run?

   (continued)

Discovering Advanced Algebra Assessment Resources B
©2004 Key Curriculum Press

Name_____ Period_____ Date_____

5. This table shows the population in 2000 for the 14 counties in Vermont.

County	2000 population
Addison	35,974
Bennington	36,994
Caledonia	29,702
Chittenden	146,571
Essex	6,459
Franklin	45,417
Grand Isle	6,901
Lamoille	23,233
Orange	28,226
Orleans	26,277
Rutland	63,400
Washington	58,039
Windham	44,216
Windsor	57,418

(*The World Almanac and Book of Facts 2002*)

a. Find the five-number summary for the data.

b. Find the range and the interquartile range (*IQR*) for the data.

c. Create a box plot of the data.

d. Are the data skewed left, skewed right, or symmetric?

e. Do the data include any outliers (values that are more than 1.5 · *IQR* from either end of the box)? If so, which counties have populations that are outliers?

6. Use the data from Problem 5.

a. Find the mean and standard deviation of the data.

b. Which counties have populations that are more than one standard deviation above or below the mean?

c. What is the percentile rank of Addison County?

d. Make a histogram of the data using an appropriate bin width.

(continued)

Name _____ Period _____ Date _____

7. Use an appropriate method to solve each system of equations.

a. $\begin{cases} y = \frac{1}{5}x + 8 \\ 3x - 3y = 24 \end{cases}$

b. $\begin{cases} -4x - 3y = -7 \\ 6x + 2y = -12 \end{cases}$

8. Consider the arithmetic sequence $-19, -12, -5, 2, 9, 16, \ldots$.

a. Write a recursive formula that describes this sequence. Use u_0 for the starting term.

b. Write an explicit formula for this sequence.

c. Determine the value of u_{27}.

d. If you were to plot the points (n, u_n) for this sequence and then draw a line through the points, what would be the slope and y-intercept of the line?

9. This table shows the amount of energy imported by the United States (including coal, natural gas, crude oil, and petroleum products) for various years.

Year	1960	1965	1970	1975	1980	1985	1990	1995	1999	2000
Energy imported (quadrillion Btu)	4.23	5.92	8.39	14.11	15.97	12.10	18.95	22.57	27.55	28.52

(*The World Almanac and Book of Facts 2002*)

a. Create a scatter plot of these data. Do these data seem linear?

b. Find the equation for the median-median line for the data. Round the slope and y-intercept to the nearest thousandth.

c. Interpret the slope of the median-median line in the context of this situation.

d. Use your median-median line to predict the amount of energy the United States will import in 2050.

e. Calculate the residuals for each data point, and find the root mean square error for your equation. Interpret the root mean square error in the context of this problem.

Discovering Advanced Algebra Assessment Resources B
©2004 Key Curriculum Press

Chapter 4 • Quiz 1

Name _____ Period _____ Date _____

1. Sketch a graph to go with the following story. Identify the variables and label your axes appropriately.

Early Saturday morning, Theo left his home and started walking to school for band practice. After walking a few blocks, he remembered that he forgot his sheet music, so he ran back home to get it. He then started out for school again, this time walking faster than before. He stopped by the bagel shop to buy some breakfast. Then he realized he was running late, so he ran as fast as he could until he arrived at school. After practice, he walked to his friend Jack's house, which was halfway between school and Theo's home.

2. Match a description with each graph.

a. 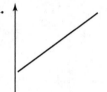   b. 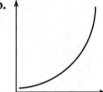   c.

A. Increasing at an increasing rate

B. Increasing at a constant rate

C. Increasing at a decreasing rate

3. Tell whether each relation is a function.

a.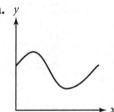

b.

$$\begin{array}{cc} x & y \\ 1 & 5 \\ 2 & 6 \\ 3 & 7 \\ 4 & 8 \end{array}$$

c. $y = 3x - 1$

4. Use the functions $f(x) = -2x + 4$ and $g(x) = \frac{x+3}{x-5}$ to find each value.

a. $f(3)$ b. $g(-6)$ c. $f(7) + f(0)$ d. x when $g(x) = 0$

Chapter 4 • Quiz 2

Name _____ Period _____ Date _____

1. The graph of $y = 6x$ is translated down 3 units and right 9 units. What is the equation of the new line?

2. The graph of $y = f(x)$ is shown below. Write an equation for each of the graphs below.

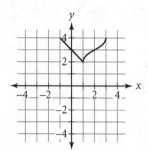

a.
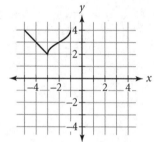

b.
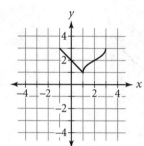

c.
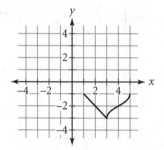

3. Describe how the graph of each function compares with the graph of $y = x^2$.

   a. $y = (x - 2)^2$ **b.** $y = (x + 5)^2 - 1$

   c. $y = -\left(x^2 + 4\right)$ **d.** $y = -x^2 + 4$

4. Each graph is a transformation of the graph of the parent function $y = \sqrt{x}$. Write an equation for each graph.

a.
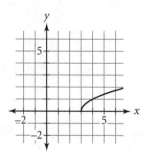

b.
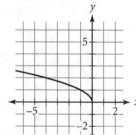

c.
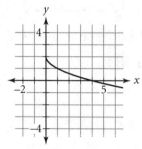

Discovering Advanced Algebra Assessment Resources B
©2004 Key Curriculum Press

Chapter 4 • Quiz 3

Name _____ Period _____ Date _____

1. Each graph is a transformation of $y = x^2$ or $y = |x|$. Write an equation for each graph.

a.

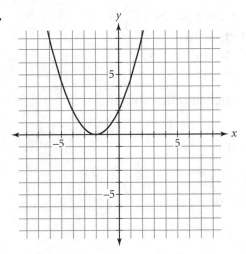

b.

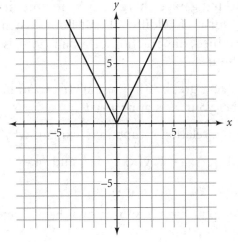

c.

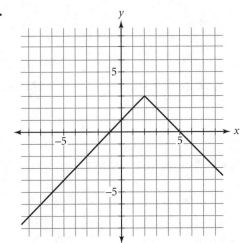

2. Write an equation for the ellipse at right. What two equations would you have to enter into your calculator to graph the ellipse?

3. Suppose $f(x) = x^2 - 5$ and $g(x) = |x + 1|$.

   a. Find $f(g(-2))$ and $g(f(-2))$.

   b. Find $f(g(x))$ and $g(f(x))$.

   c. Sketch a graph of $y = g(f(x))$.

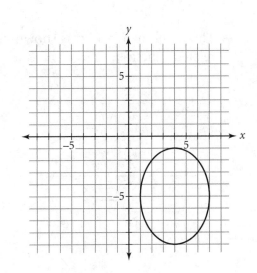

Chapter 4 • Test

Name _____ Period _____ Date _____

Answer each question and show all work clearly on a separate piece of paper.

1. A parking garage charges $3.50 for the first hour or less and then $0.50 for each additional half hour. When the parking fee is determined, any fraction of a half hour is rounded up to the next half hour.

   a. Make a graph to represent this relation. Identify the variables and label your axes appropriately.

   b. Is the relation a function? Explain why or why not.

2. If $f(x) = -\frac{x}{5} + 1$, $g(x) = 3x^2$, and $h(x) = (x - 4)^2$, find each value.

   a. $f(g(-2))$ **b.** $h(g(5))$ **c.** $g(f(x))$

3. The graph of $y = f(x)$ is shown here. Sketch the graph of each related function.

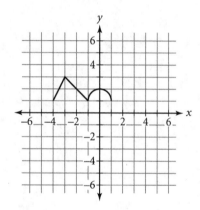

   a. $y = f(x - 3)$ **b.** $y = -f(x)$

   c. $y = f(x) - 3$ **d.** $y = 3f(x)$

4. The graph of $y = g(x)$ is shown here. Sketch the graph of each related function.

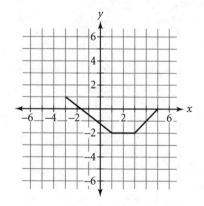

   a. $y - 2 = g(x + 3)$ **b.** $y + 3 = g(2x)$ **c.** $\dfrac{y - 1}{2} = -g(x + 1)$

                                                                               (continued)

Name_____ Period_____ Date_____

5. Find a function that fits these data.

x	-3	-1	0	1	2	5	6
y	22	7	1.75	-2	-4.25	-2	1.75

6. For each graph, name the parent function and write an equation of the graph.

a.

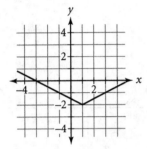

b.

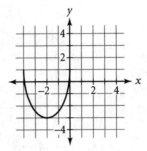

c.

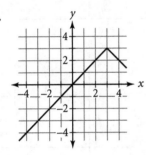

d.

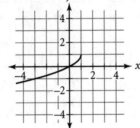

7. Solve for y.

$$\left(\frac{y}{7}\right)^2 + \left(\frac{x-1}{3}\right)^2 = 1$$

8. Solve for x.

$$\left|\frac{x+5}{2}\right| = 6$$

Chapter 4 • Constructive Assessment Options

Choose one or more of these items to replace part of the chapter test. Let students know that they will receive from 0 to 5 points for each item, depending on the correctness and completeness of their answer.

1. *(Lessons 4.3–4.6)*

Complete this chart of transformations.

Parent equation	Transformations in words	Images of (0, 0) and (1, 1)	Image equation showing transformations	Image equation solved for y
$y = x$		$(0, 0) \rightarrow$ $(1, 1) \rightarrow$	$y - 6 = x - 1$	
$y = x$	Stretch horizontally by a factor of $\frac{1}{3}$ and vertically by a factor of 2.	$(0, 0) \rightarrow$ $(1, 1) \rightarrow$		
$y = x$		$(0, 0) \rightarrow (0, 0)$ $(1, 1) \rightarrow \left(1, -\frac{2}{3}\right)$		
$y = x^2$	Reflect across the x-axis.	$(0, 0) \rightarrow$ $(1, 1) \rightarrow$		
$y = \lvert x \rvert$		$(0, 0) \rightarrow$ $(1, 1) \rightarrow$		$y = \lvert x - 4 \rvert - 6$
$y = \lvert x \rvert$	Translate left 3 units, and stretch vertically by a factor of $\frac{1}{3}$.	$(0, 0) \rightarrow$ $(1, 1) \rightarrow$		
$y = \sqrt{x}$		$(0, 0) \rightarrow$ $(1, 1) \rightarrow$	$y = \sqrt{-\frac{1}{2}x}$	
$y = \sqrt{x}$	Translate left 5 units and down 7 units.	$(0, 0) \rightarrow$ $(1, 1) \rightarrow$		

(continued)

Discovering Advanced Algebra Assessment Resources B
 ©2004 Key Curriculum Press

2. *(Lessons 4.4–4.6)*

Does the order in which you apply two transformations make a difference? Consider these four transformations.

A. Translate right 4 units and down 1 unit.

B. Reflect across the *x*-axis.

C. Stretch vertically by a factor of $\frac{1}{2}$.

D. Translate right 5 units.

a. Write the equation of each function after the given transformation has been applied. Solve each equation for *y*.

	$y = |x|$	$y = \sqrt{x}$
Apply A to the parent function.		
Apply B to the image under A.		
Apply B to the parent function.		
Apply A to the image under B.		
Apply C to the parent function.		
Apply D to the image under C.		
Apply D to the parent function.		
Apply C to the image under D.		

b. Does the order in which you apply the transformations matter? Explain.

3. *(Lesson 4.7)*

Consider the unit circle $x^2 + y^2 = 1$.

a. Write the equation of the image of the unit circle after a horizontal stretch by a factor of 4 and a vertical stretch by a factor of 4.

b. Write your equation from part a with no parentheses or fractions.

c. Graph the image. Label the coordinates of the images of the center and the intercepts.

d. Translate the image from part a left 2 units and up 3 units. Write the equation of the second image.

e. Graph the second image. Label the coordinates of the images of the original center and intercepts.

f. Find the exact coordinates of the new intercepts.

g. Write the equation of a circle with center (2, 5) and radius 3.

(continued)

4. *(Lessons 4.2, 4.8)*

The ACME Manufacturing Company makes widgets in the shape of a sector of a circle with a 60° central angle. The widgets are named by the radius of the circle from which they are stamped. The radii range from 1 millimeter to 10 centimeters. The price ACME charges for a widget depends on the surface area of the top of the widget. The price is $18 per square millimeter plus $215 for a quality check and warranty.

a. Let $A(x)$ be the function for the area of the widget in terms of its radius (in millimeters).

   i. What are the domain and range of the function?

   ii. Write an equation for the function.

   iii. Sketch a graph of $y = A(x)$.

   iv. Describe $y = A(x)$ as a transformation of its parent function.

b. Let $P(x)$ be the function for the price of a widget in terms of the surface area of its top (in square millimeters).

   i. What are the domain and range of the function?

   ii. Write the equation of the function.

   iii. Sketch a graph of $y = P(x)$.

   iv. Describe $y = P(x)$ as a transformation of its parent function.

c. Let $C(x)$ be the price of a widget in terms of its radius (in millimeters).

   i. Express $C(x)$ as a composition of the functions in parts a and b.

   ii. Write the equation for $C(x)$ with no parentheses.

   iii. What is the cost of a 4.8 mm widget? Of a 58.3 mm widget?

   iv. Sketch a graph of $y = C(x)$.

   v. Describe $y = C(x)$ as a transformation of its parent function.

Chapter 5 • Quiz 1

Name _____ **Period** _____ **Date** _____

1. Hannah paid $142,000 for a condominium. The values of the homes in the neighborhood have been appreciating by about 11% each year.

   a. If this appreciation rate continues, what will be the value of Hannah's condo in 4 years and 3 months?

   b. When will Hannah's condo be worth twice what she paid for it? (Give your answer to the nearest month.)

2. Rewrite each expression in the form ax^n.

   a. $-4x^5 \cdot 3x^{-3}$ b. $\dfrac{21x^6}{7x^{-9}}$ c. $\left(2x^8\right)^3$ d. $\left(\dfrac{x^{-2}}{5}\right)^{-1}$

3. Solve.

   a. $27 = \left(\dfrac{1}{9}\right)^x$ b. $8x^5 = 1312$ c. $\left(\sqrt[3]{x}\right)^5 = 115$

4. Consider the exponential curve with equation $y = 4 \cdot 0.6^x$.

   a. Find the y-intercept and ratio for the curve.

   b. Find another point on the curve (besides the y-intercept), and use it to write an equation for the curve in point-ratio form.

   c. Use algebra to show that the original equation and the equation you wrote in part b are equivalent. Give a reason for each step.

Chapter 5 • Quiz 2

Name _____   Period _____   Date _____

1. Radium-228 has a half-life of 5.75 years. What is the decay rate for radium-228?

2. Elly invested money in an account with a fixed interest rate. The interest is compounded annually. After 5 years her balance was $4683.79, and after 10 years her balance was $6267.97.

   a. Find an exponential equation that models these data. (Round the growth rate to hundredths.)

   b. How much did Elly originally invest?

   c. What is the interest rate for the account?

3. Find the inverse of each function, and tell whether the inverse is itself a function.

   a. $y = \dfrac{3}{8}x + 4$

   b. $y = (x + 2)^2$

   c. $(-4, -2), (-2, -1), (0, 0), (2, 1), (4, 2)$

Discovering Advanced Algebra Assessment Resources B
©2004 Key Curriculum Press

Chapter 5 • Quiz 3

Name _____   Period _____   Date _____

1. Solve. Round your answers to hundredths.

    a. $384 \cdot 10^x = 32$ b. $4^x = 224$ c. $0.7^x = 101$

2. Darius bought a flat-screen television for $2200. The value decreases by about 18% each year. How long will it take for the value to be reduced to $500?

3. Determine whether each equation is true or false. If it is false, rewrite the right side to make it true.

    a. $\log x - \log y = \log \dfrac{x}{y}$

    b. $\log x^7 = (\log x)^7$

    c. $\log_7 z = \dfrac{\log z}{\log 7}$

    d. $\log 56 = \log 7 \cdot \log 8$

4. The equation $D = 10 \log\left(\dfrac{I}{10^{-16}}\right)$ gives the intensity of a sound, D, measured in decibels (dB), where I is the power of the sound in watts per square centimeter (W/cm^2) and 10^{-16} W/cm² is the power of sound just below the threshold of hearing. A jackhammer produces sound with an intensity of 130 decibels. Find the power of the sound produced by a jackhammer.

Chapter 5 • Test

Name _____   **Period** _____   **Date** _____

Answer each question and show all work clearly on a separate piece of paper.

1. Use the properties of exponents and logarithms to rewrite each expression in another form.

    a. $m^{4/5}$ **b.** $4 \cdot \log b$ **c.** $\log_x 9$

    d. $\left(\dfrac{xy^4z^2}{xy^2z^5}\right)^{-1}$ **e.** $3^x \cdot 9^y$ **f.** $\log 7 + \log 3$

2. Solve.

    a. $6\log_{1.75} x = 24$ **b.** $\log \dfrac{x}{10^2} = -2$ **c.** $3.5x^{-4} = 175$

    d. $\sqrt[7]{x^5} = -7$ **e.** $4.5^{x^2} = 720$ **f.** $4\sqrt{3x - 9} - 7 = 17$

3. Find an equation of the exponential curve that passes through (1, 280) and (5, 17.5).

4. Armen is 25 years old now and hopes to retire when he is 60. He wants to invest $10,000 in an account so that the balance will be $80,000 when he retires. What annual percentage rate is necessary for this to happen? (Assume that the interest is compounded annually.)

5. Lucy bought a car for $25,000. The value of the car depreciates by about 13% each year. When will the value of the car be $10,000?

6. Consider the function $y = 5(x - 2)^{1/2} + 3$.

    a. Find $f^{-1}(x)$.   **b.** Find $f^{-1}(4)$.   **c.** Find $f(f^{-1}(5))$.

7. Public Service Utilities uses the equation $y = a + b\log x$ to determine the cost of electricity, where y represents the cost and x represents the time in hours. The first hour of use costs $6.75. Three hours costs $17.94.

    a. Determine the values of a and b in the model.

    b. What is the x-intercept of the graph of the model? What is the real-world meaning of the x-intercept?

    c. Use the model to find the cost for 65 hours of electricity use.

    d. If a customer can afford $15 per month for electricity, how long can he or she have the electricity turned on?

(continued)

Discovering Advanced Algebra Assessment Resources B
©2004 Key Curriculum Press

Name_____ Period_____ Date_____

8. This table shows the average per-student cost for tuition and fees for an academic year at a two-year public college.

Year	Tuition and fees
1970	$178
1980	$355
1990	$756
2000	$1627

(*The World Almanac and Book of Facts 2002*)

   a. Let x represent the number of years after 1970 and let y be the cost for tuition and fees. Plot the data on your calculator and make a sketch of the graph.

   b. Plot the graph of $(x, \log y)$ on your calculator and make a sketch of the graph. Explain how the graph provides evidence that the tuition and fees are growing exponentially.

   c. Find the median-median line for the $(x, \log y)$ data.

   d. Use your equation from part c to find a model for the original data.

   e. Use your equation from part d to estimate the cost for tuition and fees at a two-year public college in 2010.

   f. If the trend continues, when will the cost for tuition and fees first exceed $7500 per student?

   g. In 1992, the average cost for tuition and fees at a two-year college was $937. Do these data fit your model? Explain.

Chapter 5 • Constructive Assessment Options

Choose one or more of these items to replace part of the chapter test. Let students know that they will receive from 0 to 5 points for each item, depending on the correctness and completeness of their answer.

1. *(Lessons 5.1, 5.3, and 5.4)*

Over the past two decades, the number of computers in schools has been increasing. The following data show the number of students per computer in U.S. public schools. Assume that eventually there will be one student per computer.

School year	Students per computer	School year	Students per computer
1983–84	125	1992–93	16
1984–85	75	1993–94	14
1985–86	50	1994–95	10.5
1986–87	37	1995–96	10
1987–88	32	1996–97	7.8
1988–89	25	1997–98	6.1
1989–90	22	1998–99	5.7
1990–91	20	1999–2000	5.4
1991–92	18		

(World Almanac and Book of Facts 2002)

a. Find an exponential function in the form $y = ab^x$ that models the data. Let x be the number of school years after the 1983–84 school year.

b. Find an exponential function in the form $y = 1 + ab^x$ (that is, an exponential function with a long-run value of 1) that models the data.

c. Which model do you think better represents this situation? Explain.

d. Using the better model, predict the number of students per computer in the 2005–06 school year.

e. Based on the better model, in what year will the number of students per computer first be less than 2? Explain how you found your answer.

(continued)

Discovering Advanced Algebra Assessment Resources B
©2004 Key Curriculum Press

2. *(Lessons 5.1–5.3, 5.6, 5.7)*

When is a stretch equivalent to a translation? Consider the function $y = ab^x$.

a. Show algebraically that a vertical stretch of the function by a factor of b is equivalent to translation left by 1 unit. Give a reason for each step.

b. Describe a transformation of $y = a(2)^x$ that is equivalent to a vertical stretch by a factor of 4. Use algebra to justify your answer.

c. Describe a transformation of $y = a(2)^x$ that is equivalent to a vertical stretch by a factor of p. Use algebra to justify your answer. (Hint: You will need to write p as 2 raised to a power.)

d. Describe a transformation of $y = ab^x$ that is equivalent to a vertical stretch by a factor of p. Use algebra to justify your answer.

3. *(Lessons 5.1–5.7)*

Consider the function $f(x) = -2^{-0.8x-10} + 12$.

a. Enter $f(x)$ as Y1 on your calculator and sketch the graph of the function.

b. What are the domain and range of the function?

c. Use algebra to find the *exact* values of the x- and y-intercepts. Show all your work. Trace the graph to check your results.

d. Describe $f(x)$ as a transformation of the parent function $y = 2^x$.

e. The point $(0, 1)$ is on the parent function. Find the image of this point on $y = f(x)$.

f. Find $f^{-1}(x)$. Enter it as Y2 on your calculator and sketch its graph.

g. What are the domain and range of $f^{-1}(x)$?

h. Enter $f^{-1}(f(x))$ as Y3 on your calculator (that is, Y2(Y1(X))) and enter $f(f^{-1}(x))$ as Y4 (that is, Y1(Y2(X))). Compare the graphs of Y3 and Y4.

(continued)

4. *(Lessons 5.6–5.8)*

The Richter scale is a logarithmic scale used to measure the magnitudes of earthquakes. The Richter magnitude, M, of an earthquake with intensity I is given by the formula $M = \log \frac{I}{I_0}$, where I_0 is the intensity of the smallest earthquake that can be measured. In parts a–c, show all your work.

a. The San Francisco earthquake of 1906 measured 7.7 on the Richter scale. An earthquake in Napa Valley, California, in 2000 measured 4.9. How many times more intense was the San Francisco earthquake than the Napa Valley earthquake?

b. The largest earthquake of the 20th century was in Chile in 1960. It was 63 times more intense than the 1906 San Francisco earthquake. What was the Richter magnitude of the earthquake in Chile?

c. A blast at a construction site has a Richter magnitude of about 1.0. About how many construction site blasts would it take to have an intensity equivalent to the 1960 earthquake in Chile?

Chapter 6 • Quiz 1

Name _____ **Period** _____ **Date** _____

1. On the last two math tests, all the students in Ms. Brady's first-period class received A's, B's, or C's.

   • Of the students who got A's on the first test, 60% also got A's on the second test, 20% got B's, and 20% got C's.

   • Of the students who got B's on the first test, 25% got A's on the second test, 75% got B's again, and 0% got C's.

   • Of the students who got C's on the first test, 10% got A's on the second test, 40% got B's, and 50% got C's again.

   a. Draw and label a transition diagram to represent this situation.

   b. Write a transition matrix to represent this situation. Label the matrix so it is clear what the rows and columns represent.

2. Complete the following matrix arithmetic problems. If a problem is impossible, explain why.

   a. $\begin{bmatrix} 1 & 3 \\ -4 & 1 \\ 1 & 7 \end{bmatrix} \begin{bmatrix} 2 & -2 \\ 3 & 7 \\ 12 & 0 \end{bmatrix}$

   b. $\begin{bmatrix} 2 & -6 \\ -3 & 3 \end{bmatrix} - \begin{bmatrix} -9 & 4 \\ 5 & -3 \end{bmatrix}$

   c. $-5 \begin{bmatrix} 1 & 8 & -2 & 1 & 0 \\ 3 & 5 & 0 & -4 & 6 \end{bmatrix}$

   d. $\begin{bmatrix} 2 & 0 & 11 \end{bmatrix} \begin{bmatrix} -5 & 2 \\ 7 & 2 \\ 2 & -1 \end{bmatrix}$

Chapter 6 • Quiz 2

Name _____ Period _____ Date _____

1. Tickets to the school musical cost $3 for students and $5 for nonstudents. For Friday night's performance, the total ticket sales were $1790. The number of student tickets sold was 100 less than twice the number of nonstudent tickets sold.

   a. Write a system of equations to represent this situation. Tell what the variables represent.

   b. Solve the system of equations using the row reduction method. How many student tickets were sold? How many nonstudent tickets were sold?

2. Solve this system by using an inverse matrix. Show your work.

$$\begin{cases} 2x + 5y + z = 1 \\ x - 3y + 2z = 16 \\ -x + 2y - 3z = -17 \end{cases}$$

3. Solve this system using any method. Show your work.

$$\begin{cases} 6x - 2y + z = -18 \\ x - y + z = -1 \\ -7x + 5y - 3z = 19 \end{cases}$$

Discovering Advanced Algebra Assessment Resources B
©2004 Key Curriculum Press

Chapter 6 • Quiz 3

Name _____   Period _____   Date _____

1. Sketch the feasible region for this system of inequalities. Find the coordinates of each vertex.

$$\begin{cases} y \geq 1 \\ x \leq 2 \\ -x + 2y \leq 6 \\ x + 2y \geq 2 \end{cases}$$

2. For the system in Problem 1, find the vertex that maximizes each expression.

   a. $2x + 2y$ b. $3x - y$ c. $6x - 2y$

3. Monica is growing carrots and tomatoes in a community garden. She has a total of 250 ft² to grow them in. She wants to use more area for tomatoes than for carrots, but she doesn't want to use more than 160 ft² for tomatoes. Find the maximum area Monica can use for carrots.

Chapter 6 • Test

Name _____ Period _____ Date _____

Answer each question and show all work clearly on a separate piece of paper.

1. Use these matrices to do the following arithmetic problems. If a problem is impossible, explain why.

$$[A] = [5 \quad -2 \quad 3] \qquad [B] = \begin{bmatrix} -2 & 3 \\ 1 & 6 \\ 0 & -1 \end{bmatrix}$$

$$[C] = \begin{bmatrix} -3 & 2 \\ -2 & 3 \end{bmatrix} \qquad [D] = \begin{bmatrix} -1 & 0 \\ 9 & 3 \end{bmatrix}$$

   a. $[A][B]$ b. $[D] - [C]$ c. $2[B][C]$

   d. $[B][B]$ e. $-3[C] + 2[D]$

2. Solve this system by using row reduction.
$$\begin{cases} 2x = 10 - 5y \\ 3 - 7x = 14 + 6y \end{cases}$$

3. Solve this system by using an inverse matrix.
$$\begin{cases} 8x + 2y + z = 0 \\ -2x - 4y + 3z = 1 \\ 5x + 6y + 2z = 16 \end{cases}$$

4. Consider this system of inequalities.
$$\begin{cases} y \le 4 \\ y \ge 1 \\ y > 2 - 2x \\ 3x + 4y < 16 \end{cases}$$

   a. Graph the feasible region and find its vertices.

   b. Find the value in the feasible region that minimizes the value of the expression $2x - 5y$.

   c. Find the value in the feasible region that maximizes the value of the expression $x + y$.

(continued)

Discovering Advanced Algebra Assessment Resources B
©2004 Key Curriculum Press

Name_____ Period_____ Date_____

5. Science University offers only three majors: biology, chemistry, and physics. In the freshman class this year, there were 580 biology majors, 640 chemistry majors, and 360 physics majors. Students at SU switch majors frequently. Each year

   • 10% of the biology majors switch to chemistry, 10% switch to physics, and the rest stay with biology.

   • 15% of the chemistry majors switch to biology, 25% switch to physics, and the rest stay with chemistry.

   • 20% of the physics majors switch to biology, 30% switch to chemistry, and the rest stay with physics.

   a. Draw a transition diagram for this situation.

   b. Write and label a transition matrix for this situation. List the majors in the order biology, chemistry, physics.

   c. When this year's freshmen are sophomores, about how many will be biology majors? Chemistry majors? Physics majors? (Assume no one drops out.)

   d. By the time this year's freshmen are seniors, about how many will be in each major? (Again, assume no one drops out.)

6. The Pizza Shack is famous for its thick-crust pizza. Last Wednesday, the Divita, Lee, and Washington families all ate at the Pizza Shack.

   • The Divitas ordered a cheese pizza with pepperoni and mushrooms, a cheese pizza with garlic and olives, and five soft drinks. Their bill was $30.75.

   • The Lees ordered a cheese pizza with sausage, onions, and green peppers and three soft drinks. Their bill was $17.50.

   • The Washingtons were having a birthday party. They ordered five cheese pizzas, three with just pepperoni and two with pineapple and Canadian bacon. They also ordered 12 soft drinks. Their bill was $71.75.

   Write and solve a system of equations to find the price of a plain cheese pizza, the price of each topping, and the price of a soft drink. (Assume that the price for each topping is the same and that the bills do not include tax or tip.)

Chapter 6 • Constructive Assessment Options

Choose one or more of these items to replace part of the chapter test. Let students know that they will receive from 0 to 5 points for each item, depending on the correctness and completeness of their answer.

1. *(Lessons 6.1, 6.2)*

Three types of cars—the Aries, the Dinky, and the Putter—are each produced by assembly plants in Queenston, Sherry, and Lint. Matrix [A] shows the number of each model produced last week at each plant.

$$[A] = \begin{bmatrix} 45 & 20 & 32 \\ 15 & 52 & 22 \\ 38 & 28 & 19 \end{bmatrix} \begin{matrix} \text{Queenston} \\ \text{Sherry} \\ \text{Lint} \end{matrix}$$

with columns labeled Aries, Dinky, Putter

Teams of workers assemble each car in three stages: chassis assembly, parts assembly, and final assembly. Matrix [B] shows the team hours needed for each assembly stage for one car of each type.

$$[B] = \begin{bmatrix} 4 & 6 & 3 \\ 2 & 5 & 4 \\ 5 & 3 & 4 \end{bmatrix} \begin{matrix} \text{Aries} \\ \text{Dinky} \\ \text{Putter} \end{matrix}$$

with columns labeled Chassis, Parts, Final

a. Explain the meaning of each matrix product. You do not have to find the actual product.

    i. $[1 \quad 1 \quad 1][A]$
    ii. $[A]\begin{bmatrix} 1 \\ 1 \\ 1 \end{bmatrix}$
    iii. $[A][B]$

b. Write a matrix product (like those in part a) to represent

    i. the total number of team hours needed to assemble one car of each type

    ii. the total number of hours spent last week in all plants on each assembly stage

c. The company makes a profit of $4000 on each Aries, $3500 on each Dinky, and $2800 on each Putter. Write a profit matrix, [P], and write a matrix product that would give the total weekly profit for each plant.

d. Explain how you could use matrix multiplication to find the total profits from each type of car last week. (You may introduce a new matrix or use only the matrices from the previous steps.)

(continued)

2. *(Lessons 6.3, 6.4)*

Consider the sequence 4, 6, 12, 22, ...

a. Describe, in words, a rule that generates the sequence.

b. Find the next three terms of the sequence.

c. Find a recursive rule to generate the sequence. (Assume that the first term is u_1.)

d. The sequence can be generated by a function in the form $f(n) = an^2 + bn + c$. Use matrices to find a, b, and c. Show all your work.

3. *(Lessons 6.5, 6.6)*

Whatnot Manufacturing makes widgets and gizmos. Each widget takes 6 minutes to cut out and 9 minutes to wire. Each gizmo takes 5 minutes to cut out and 15 minutes to wire. The cutout machine can only be used 7 hours a day, and the two people who do the wiring can only work a combined total of 13 hours a day. At least 3 widgets must be produced for every 7 gizmos produced. The company makes a daily profit of $3.50 for each widget it produces and a profit of $6.50 for each gizmo it produces. Let w be the number of widgets produced and g be the number of gizmos produced.

a. Write an inequality to describe the cutout time constraint.

b. Write an inequality to describe the wiring time constraint.

c. Write an inequality to describe the ratio of widgets to gizmos constraint.

d. Write inequalities for two commonsense constraints.

e. Graph the inequalities from parts a–d, and identify each vertex of the feasible region.

f. Write an equation for the profit P. How many widgets and how many gizmos should be made to yield the maximum daily profit? What is the maximum daily profit?

Chapters 4–6 • Exam

Name _____ **Period** _____ **Date** _____

1. The graph of $y = f(x)$ is shown here.

   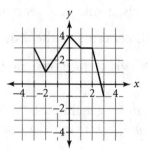

   a. Find $f(-3)$.

   b. Find all x for which $f(x) = 3$.

   c. What are the domain and range of f?

   d. Sketch a graph of the inverse of f.

   e. Is the inverse of f a function? Explain why or why not.

2. Solve each equation. Round your answer to the nearest hundredth.

   a. $16(0.82)^x = 12$

   b. $\log_6 360 = x$

   c. $\log 133 - \log 7 = \log x$

   d. $\sqrt[5]{2x - 17} + 21 = 24$

   e. $\log x^4 = 12$

3. Rewrite each expression in the form ax^n.

   a. $\left(-3x^{-1}x^4\right)^3$

   b. $\left(\dfrac{8x^{-3}x^6}{(5x)^2}\right)^{-1}$

   c. $\sqrt[3]{64x^5}$

4. Find the product

$$\begin{bmatrix} -4 & 2 & 0 \\ 0 & -1 & 3 \\ 5 & 2 & 7 \end{bmatrix} \begin{bmatrix} 2 & -1 \\ 7 & 0 \\ 1 & 3 \end{bmatrix}.$$

5. Each graph is a transformation of the graph of $y = x^2$, $y = |x|$, or $x^2 + y^2 = 1$. Write an equation for each graph.

   a.

   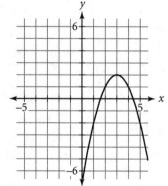

   b.

   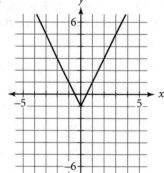

   c.

   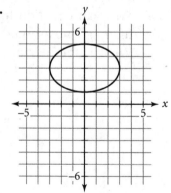

(continued)

Discovering Advanced Algebra Assessment Resources B
©2004 Key Curriculum Press

Name_____ Period_____ Date_____

6. Meg has three dogs—Skippy, Gizmo, and Chopper. The sum of the dogs' weights is 166 pounds. If you add three times Skippy's weight to Gizmo's weight, the sum is 2 pounds more than Chopper's weight. If you subtract three-fourths of Skippy's weight from four times Gizmo's weight, the result is equal to twice Chopper's weight. How much does each dog weigh?

7. Consider this system of inequalities.

$$\begin{cases} y > -x \\ y + 4 \le \frac{4}{3}x \\ y \ge -3 \\ y \le -4x + 12 \end{cases}$$

a. Graph the feasible region and find the coordinates of its vertices.

b. Find the point in the feasible region that maximizes the value of $-2x - 3y$.

8. Milo invested some money in an account that earned a fixed-percent interest compounded annually. After 4 years, his investment was worth $4254.27. After 6 years, it was worth $4690.33.

a. What is the annual interest rate for Milo's investment?

b. How much did Milo initially invest?

c. How many years will it take for the value of Milo's investment to triple?

Chapter 7 • Quiz 1

Name _____ Period _____ Date _____

1. Find a polynomial function that models these data.

x	1	2	3	4	5	6
y	−7	−6	−1	8	21	38

2. Find the roots of each equation.

   a. $(x - 2)(x + 11) = 0$ b. $7x(12x - 3) = 0$ c. $x^2 - 5x = 0$

3. Find the equation of this parabola in vertex form and factored form.

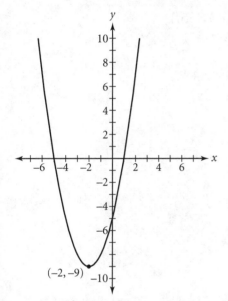

4. Convert each quadratic function to vertex form. Identify the vertex.

   a. $y = x^2 + 12x + 35$ b. $y = -5x^2 - 20x + 12$

Chapter 7 • Quiz 2

Name _____ Period _____ Date _____

1. Roscoe hit a ball straight up at a speed of 110 ft/s. His bat hit the ball at a height 3 ft above the ground. After how many seconds did the ball hit the ground? (Give your answer to the nearest hundredth of a second.)

2. Find each sum or difference.

   a. $(-2 + 6i) + (5 - 3i)$

   b. $(11 + i) - (3 - 4i)$

3. Find each product or quotient.

   a. $\dfrac{4 + 6i}{2 - 2i}$

   b. $(3 - 5i)(3 + 5i)$

4. Find the exact solutions to each equation.

   a. $x^2 + 8 = 0$

   b. $x^2 + 2 = -4x$

Discovering Advanced Algebra Assessment Resources B
©2004 Key Curriculum Press

Chapter 7 • Quiz 3

Name _____ Period _____ Date _____

1. Write an equation in factored form for a polynomial function with real coefficients, x-intercepts -2, 2, and 6, and y-intercept -96.

2. Write an equation in general form for a polynomial function with real coefficients and zeros at $x = 4$ and $x = 1 + 3i$.

3. Find the roots of the polynomial equation $7x^3 + 5x^2 - 49x - 35 = 0$.

4. Write the equation of the graph in factored form.

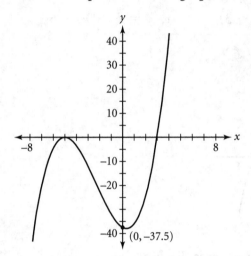

Chapter 7 • Test

Name _____ Period _____ Date _____

Answer each question and show all work clearly on a separate piece of paper.

1. Solve.

   a. $2x^2 = 30 - 4x$ **b.** $x^3 + 8x = -6x^2$

2. Tell whether each equation is written in general form, vertex form, or factored form. Write each equation in the other two forms.

   a. $y = 5(x - 2)^2 - 3$ **b.** $y = -3(x - 4)(x - 3)$ **c.** $y = x^2 - 4x + 6$

3. Write the equation of each graph in factored form.

   a. 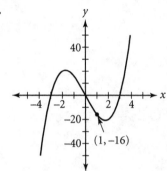   **b.**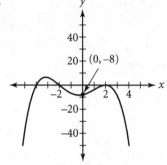

4. Consider this sequence of squares made from smaller squares. Each of the smaller squares has side length 1 unit.

   a. The square with side length 2 units contains four 1-by-1 squares and one 2-by-2 square, for a total of five squares. Complete the table below to show the total number of squares contained inside the squares with side lengths 3 units and 4 units.

Side length	1	2	3	4	5
Number of squares	1	5			55

   b. How many squares would be contained in a square with side length 6 units?

   c. Use finite differences to find the degree of the polynomial that models these data.

(continued)

Discovering Advanced Algebra Assessment Resources B
©2004 Key Curriculum Press

Name _____ Period _____ Date _____

5. Consider the polynomial function

$P(x) = 3x^4 - 4x^3 - 6x^2 + 20x - 16$

a. List all possible rational zeros of the function.

b. Find all the rational zeros.

c. Find any other zeros.

d. Write the equation of $P(x)$ in factored form.

6. Eli stands on a balcony of a tall building and throws a tennis ball straight up at a speed of 14 m/s. He releases the tennis ball at a height of 60 m from the ground. In parts a–c, round your answers to the nearest hundredth.

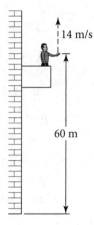

14 m/s

60 m

a. When does the tennis ball hit the ground?

b. When does the tennis ball pass the point from which it was released?

c. What is the maximum height reached by the ball? When does it reach this height?

7. Write an equation in general form for a 4th-degree polynomial with real coefficients, zeros $-i$ and $-4i$, and y-intercept 40.

8. Graph the function $y = -x^4 - 5x^3 + 4x^2 + 20x$ on your calculator. Sketch the graph. Describe the end behavior and identify the intercepts and extreme values. Round values to the nearest tenth.

Chapter 7 • Constructive Assessment Options

Choose one or more of these items to replace part of the chapter test. Let students know that they will receive from 0 to 5 points for each item, depending on the correctness and completeness of their answer.

1. *(Lesson 7.1)*

   A heavy object was dropped from a third-story balcony. The table below shows the distance the object fell every half second after it was dropped.

Time (s)	0.5	1.0	1.5	2.0	2.5	3.0
Distance (m)	1.23	4.90	11.03	19.60	30.63	44.10

   a. Use the finite differences method to determine which type of function models these data.

   b. Find a model for the data values by choosing three *consecutive* data pairs, using them to write a system of equations, and then solving the system.

   c. Repeat part b, but this time use three pairs of values spread over the range of the data.

   d. Examine and compare the models you found in parts b and c. Which do you feel is a better model for the data? Give reasons to support your choice.

2. *(Lessons 7.4, 7.5)*

   In a baseball game, the center fielder throws the ball to home plate so that the ball reaches the plate just in time for the catcher to tag the sliding runner. The height of the throw is modeled by the function $h(t) = -4.9t^2 + 20t + 1.3$, where t is the time after the ball is released in seconds and $h(t)$ is the height of the ball in meters.

   a. Find $h(0)$ and explain what the value means in the context of this problem.

   b. How long does it take the ball to reach the plate? Show and explain your work.

   c. What is the maximum height of the ball? When is the maximum height reached? Show and explain your work.

   d. The runner on third base hesitates for half a second and then sprints the 90 ft to home plate, arriving at exactly the same time as the ball. What is the runner's speed in meters per second? Explain how you found your answer. (*Note:* 1 in. = 2.54 cm.)

   e. Graph $y = h(t)$. Is the graph a good picture of the path of the ball? Explain.

(continued)

3. *(Lessons 7.2, 7.3, 7.7)*

You can create a box from a 24-by-60-unit sheet of cardboard by using the pattern below. The box will have a lid with a flap that tucks in to keep the box closed. To form the box, you cut along the solid lines and fold along the dashed lines.

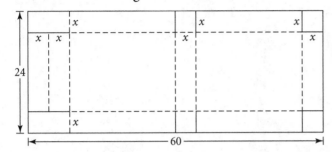 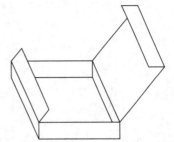

a. What will the dimensions of the box be?

b. Write a function in both factored form and general form for the volume of the box in terms of x.

c. What is a meaningful domain for the volume function? Explain.

d. Trace a graph or zoom in on a table to find the maximum possible volume.

e. To the nearest thousandth of a unit, find the dimensions of the box or boxes that fit this pattern and that have volume 1000 cubic units.

f. Let a and b be the dimensions of the sheet of cardboard. Assume $a \le b$. Write a function in both factored and general form for the volume of the box in terms of x.

g. Give a meaningful domain for the general volume function. Explain.

4. *(Lesson 7.6)*

In parts a–f, find z, and then find the indicated roots of z. Plot the roots on a complex plane.

a. $(-3)^2 = z$

$\sqrt{z} = $ _____

b. $(5i)^2 = z$

$\sqrt{z} = $ _____

c. $(-1 + i\sqrt{3})^3 = z$

$\sqrt[3]{z} = $ _____

d. $\left(\frac{1}{2} + \frac{\sqrt{3}}{2}i\right)^3 = z$

$\sqrt[3]{z} = $ _____

e. $(1 + i)^4 = z$

$\sqrt[4]{z} = $ _____

f. $(2i)^4 = z$

$\sqrt[4]{z} = $ _____

g. Describe any patterns you notice in your results for parts a–f.

Chapter 8 • Quiz 1

Name _____ Period _____ Date _____

1. Graph each pair of parametric equations, and use arrows to indicate the direction of increasing t-values. Limit the t-values as indicated. Use a t-step of 0.5 or less.

   a. $x = 2t - 3$
   $y = -3t + 4$
   $-1 \leq t \leq 3$

   b. $x = t^2 + 1$
   $y = t - 1$
   $-2 \leq t \leq 2$

2. Write each pair of parametric equations in Problem 1 as a single equation in x and y.

3. Consider the graph below.

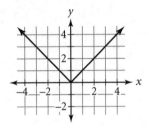

   a. Write a pair of parametric equations for the graph.

   b. Write a pair of parametric equations that will translate the graph left 3 units and stretch it vertically by a factor of 2.

Chapter 8 • Quiz 2

Name _____   Period _____   Date _____

1. Find c to the nearest tenth of a unit.

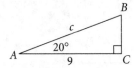
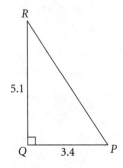

2. Find the measure of $\angle P$.

3. A ship leaves Beachville and travels on a bearing of 245° directly toward Port City, 228 miles away. The ship is traveling at a speed of 24 mi/h.

   a. How long will it take the ship to reach Port City?

   b. To the nearest mile, how far west and how far south is Port City from Beachville?

4. Suppose you want to row your boat across a 3-mile-wide river. You can row at a speed of 2.5 mi/h. The current is flowing south at a rate of 1.4 mi/h. At what angle upstream should you aim your boat so that it ends up going straight across?

5. The motion of a projectile is described by the equations

$$x = 72t\cos 29°$$
$$y = -16t^2 + 72t\sin 29° + 5.5$$

   a. From what height and at what angle was the projectile released?

   b. What was the initial velocity of the projectile?

   c. Describe the position of the projectile 1.5 s after it was released.

Discovering Advanced Algebra Assessment Resources B
©2004 Key Curriculum Press

Chapter 8 • Quiz 3

Name _____ **Period** _____ **Date** _____

1. Find the unknown lengths m and n to the nearest tenth of a unit.

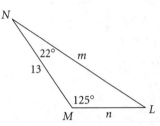

2. Find all the angle measures to the nearest degree.

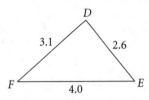

3. Ship A is 4.5 miles from a lighthouse at a bearing of 160°. Ship B is 7 miles from the lighthouse at a bearing of 260°. To the nearest tenth of a mile, how far apart are the ships?

Chapter 8 • Test

Name _____ Period _____ Date _____

Answer each question and show all work clearly on a separate piece of paper.

1. Consider the parametric equations $x = \sqrt{0.5t}$ and $y = t - 2$.

   a. Sketch a graph of the equations for $-2 \le t \le 5$. Use arrows to indicate the direction of increasing t-values.

   b. Eliminate the parameter to get a single equation in x and y.

   c. Sketch a graph of the equation you found in part b. How does the graph compare with the graph you sketched in part a? Explain any differences.

2. Consider the graph below.

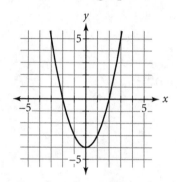

   a. Write a pair of parametric equations for the graph.

   b. Write a pair of parametric equations that would reflect the graph across the x-axis.

   c. Write a pair of parametric equations that would stretch the original graph horizontally by a factor of 2.

   d. Write a pair of parametric equations that would translate the original graph right 2 units and then reflect the result across the y-axis.

3. Find x. Round angle measures to whole degrees and lengths to tenths.

   a.
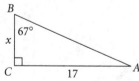

   b.

   c.
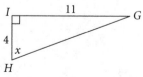

   d.
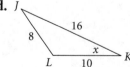

(continued)

Discovering Advanced Algebra Assessment Resources B
©2004 Key Curriculum Press

Name _____ Period _____ Date _____

4. A football player kicks a ball from a tee on the ground 40 yd from the goalpost. The ball leaves his foot at an angle of 34° and a velocity of 71 ft/s and heads straight toward the goalpost. For the kick to be good, it must pass over the crossbar of the goalpost, which is 10 ft off the ground.

   a. Is the kick good? How many feet above or below the crossbar does the ball pass?

   b. How far does the ball travel horizontally before it hits the ground?

5. Ship A and ship B leave the town of Seaside at the same time. Ship A travels on a bearing of 55° at a speed of 22 mi/h. Ship B travels on a bearing of 280° at a speed of 19 mi/h.

   a. For each ship, write a pair of parametric equations giving the ship's position relative to Seaside at time t.

   b. When ship A is 75 miles north of Seaside, how far east of Seaside is it? What is ship B's position at this time? Give your answers to the nearest mile.

   c. After 6 hours, how far apart are the two ships? Give your answer to the nearest mile.

6. A pilot flies due south from city A to city B. The cities are 700 miles apart, and the pilot sets the plane's controls to fly at 190 mi/h. Winds are blowing directly from the east at a speed of 17 mi/h. To the nearest hundredth of a degree, what bearing should the pilot set so that the plane lands in city B?

Chapter 8 • Constructive Assessment Options

Choose one or more of these items to replace part of the chapter test. Let students know that they will receive from 0 to 5 points for each item, depending on the correctness and completeness of their answer.

1. *(Lessons 8.3, 8.6)*

Sharon and Wanda are on the final leg of an orienteering race. They are traveling at about 2 km/h through the woods. It is 1:00 P.M., and they must phone race headquarters now and predict the time they will get back to their base camp. If they finish within 15 minutes of the predicted time, they will receive 50 bonus points. If they finish before 3:30, they will receive 100 bonus points.

Sharon and Wanda know that the base camp is on a bearing of 35° from their present position. They can see that the fire tower, which is visible for 10 km from any direction, is due north of where they are standing. They estimate that it is about 6.5 km away. They also remember that when they hiked through the woods from the base camp to the fire tower, it took them 2 hours.

  a. Draw a diagram of this situation, labeling all the angles and distances you know.

  b. How far are Sharon and Wanda from their base camp? Show and explain your work. If there is more than one possible answer, give all the possibilities.

  c. What additional information should Sharon and Wanda try to recall? How would this information be helpful?

  d. What time estimate should Sharon and Wanda give for their arrival? Explain your reasoning.

2. *(Lessons 8.3, 8.7)*

Seth has 20 m of fencing. He wants to build a pen in which one side is twice as long as the other, with the angle between the two sides measuring 40°.

  a. How long should each side of the pen be? Show and explain your work.

  b. What will be the area of the finished pen? Show and explain your work.

(continued)

Discovering Advanced Algebra Assessment Resources B
©2004 Key Curriculum Press

3. *(Lessons 8.4, 8.5)*

A pitcher pitches a ball to home plate from a height of 5 ft at angle θ. The initial velocity of the ball is 70 mi/h. The pitcher is 60 ft from the plate.

  a. Write parametric equations to model the pitch. Assume that the pitcher is not standing on a mound.

  b. The strike zone is between 2 and 4.5 ft above the plate. Plot two points on your calculator to represent the upper and lower limits of the strike zone.

  c. Experiment with various values of θ to find the range of values that will result in a strike.

  d. The pitcher's next pitch is a fastball with an initial velocity of 90 mi/h. Find the range of θ-values that will result in a strike for the pitch.

  e. Comment on your results from parts c and d.

Chapter 9 • Quiz 1

Name _____ Period _____ Date _____

1. Find the equation of the locus of points that are equidistant from the points $(2, -5)$ and $(1, 3)$.

2. A circle has center $(-3, 4)$ and passes through the point $(-1, 2)$. Write both standard and parametric equations for the circle.

3. Write an equation in standard form for the graph below, and give the exact coordinates of the foci.

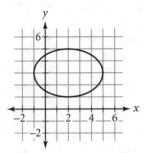

Chapter 9 • Quiz 2

Name _____ **Period** _____ **Date** _____

1. Write an equation for the parabola with focus $(2, -3)$ and directrix $x = 4$.

2. Sketch a graph of the hyperbola and give the exact coordinates of the foci.

   $$(x - 3)^2 - \left(\frac{y}{2}\right)^2 = 1$$

3. Write the equation in standard form, and describe the shape and key features of its graph.

   $$9x^2 + 16y^2 + 36x - 160y + 292 = 0$$

4. Write an equation for the graph in standard form.

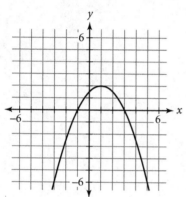

Discovering Advanced Algebra Assessment Resources B
©2004 Key Curriculum Press

Chapter 9 • Quiz 3

Name _____ **Period** _____ **Date** _____

1. Describe how the function has been transformed from the parent function $y = \frac{1}{x}$.

$$y = \frac{5x - 32}{x - 7}$$

2. Describe the asymptotes, holes, and intercepts of the graph of

$$y = \frac{2x^2 - 10x}{x^2 - 3x - 10}$$

3. Add.

$$\frac{x + 7}{x^2 - x - 6} + \frac{2}{x^2 - 6x + 9}$$

4. Divide.

$$\frac{2x - 10}{x^2 - 3x - 10} \div \frac{4x - 20}{x^2 + 3x + 2}$$

Chapter 9 • Test

Name _____ Period _____ Date _____

Answer each question and show all work clearly on a separate piece of paper.

In Problems 1–3, convert the equation to standard form and then sketch its graph. Plot and label foci, directrices, and asymptotes where appropriate.

1. $x^2 + y^2 + 8x - 6y + 21 = 0$

2. $-9x^2 + 4y^2 - 54x - 117 = 0$

3. $x^2 - 2x + 5y + 1 = 0$

4. Suppose you have 180 mL of a solution that is 60% acid and 40% water. How much acid do you need to add to make a solution that is 75% acid?

5. Write an equation for an ellipse with center $(-2, -2)$, major axis of length 10, and foci at $(-2, -5)$ and $(-2, 1)$.

6. Write an equation for a parabola with focus $(3, 1)$ and directrix $y = -3$.

7. Write an equation for the hyperbola below.

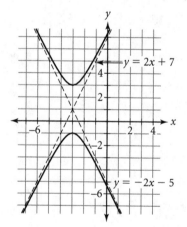

8. Graph the equation.

$$y = \frac{x^2 - 7x + 12}{x - 3}$$

9. Describe the features of the graph of

$$y = \frac{x^2 - 3x - 10}{x^2 + 10x + 25}$$

10. Perform the indicated operation. Give the result in factored form.

a. $\dfrac{1}{x^2 + 2x - 15} - \dfrac{3}{x^2 + 9x + 20}$

b. $\dfrac{x^2 + 9x + 8}{x^2 - 6x + 8} \div \dfrac{x^2 + 16x + 64}{x^2 + 4x - 32}$

Discovering Advanced Algebra Assessment Resources B
©2004 Key Curriculum Press

Chapter 9 • Constructive Assessment Options

Choose one or more of these items to replace part of the chapter test.
Let students know that they will receive from 0 to 5 points for each
item, depending on the correctness and completeness of their answer.

1. *(Lessons 9.2, 9.3, 9.5)*
Consider the equations $x^2 - y + 1 = 0$ and $9x^2 + 4y^2 - 36 = 0$.
Complete parts a–c without using a graphing calculator.

  a. Describe the graphs of the two equations, identifying the defining
features of each.

  b. Sketch the graphs of both equations on the same set of axes. How
many points of intersection do they have?

  c. Find the point(s) of intersection algebraically. Explain your
procedure.

  d. Write the equations in parametric form and graph them on
the same calculator screen. Trace the graph to verify that the
intersection points you found in part c are correct.

2. *(Lessons 9.1, 9.3, 9.8)*
In a parabola, the length of the chord through the focus and
perpendicular to the axis of symmetry is a measure of the width
of the parabola.

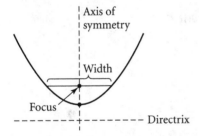

  a. A parabola has focus (2, 4) and directrix $y = 2$. Write the equation
of the parabola in vertex form, and find the width. Explain all your
work (both how you found the equation and how you found the
width).

  b. A parabola has focus (2, 4) and directrix $y = -4$. Write the
equation of the parabola in vertex form, and find the width.

  c. A parabola has focus (a, b) and directrix $y = c$. Write the equation
of the parabola in vertex form, and find the width. Explain all your
work.

  d. Make a conjecture about the width of a parabola.

(continued)

3. *(Lessons 9.6–9.8)*

The total resistance, R_T, in ohms, Ω, of an electrical circuit with three parallel paths can be calculated by using the formula $\frac{1}{R_T} = \frac{1}{R_1} + \frac{1}{R_2} + \frac{1}{R_3}$, where R_1, R_2, and R_3 are the resistances of paths 1, 2, and 3, respectively.

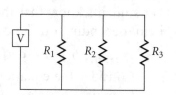

a. Find the total resistance of a three-path circuit in which $R_1 = 24 \ \Omega$, $R_2 = 30 \ \Omega$, and $R_3 = 60 \ \Omega$. Show your work.

b. The total resistance, R_T, of a three-path circuit is 32 Ω, and you also know that $R_1 = 64 \ \Omega$ and $R_2 = R_3$. Find R_2. Show your work.

In a circuit for her personal robot, Roberta has determined that $R_1 = 2R_2$ and $R_3 = R_1 - 16 \ \Omega$.

c. If $R_T = 20 \ \Omega$, find R_1, R_2, and R_3. Show your work.

d. Suppose Roberta does not know R_T for the circuit. Express R_T as a rational function of one of the resistances R_1, R_2, or R_3.

e. Graph your function from part d in the window [0, 50, 10, 0, 30, 10].

f. Graph $R_T = 20 \ \Omega$ in the same widow as the function in part e, and trace the graph to find the intersection(s) of the two graphs.

g. Check that one of your answers in part f matches your answer to part c. Explain why the other intersection has no real-world meaning.

4. *(Lesson 9.7)*

Consider the function

$$f(x) = \frac{-2(x^2 - 4)}{x^2 + 2x - 3}$$

Complete parts a–g without using a graphing calculator.

a. Find any x-intercepts of $f(x)$.

b. Find any vertical asymptotes of $f(x)$.

c. Identify any other asymptotes.

d. Sketch a graph of $f(x)$.

e. What are the domain and range of $f(x)$?

f. For which x-values is $f(x)$ positive? For which x-values is $f(x)$ negative?

g. Over what domain interval(s) is $f(x)$ an increasing function? For what domain intervals is $f(x)$ a decreasing function?

Discovering Advanced Algebra Assessment Resources B
©2004 Key Curriculum Press

Chapters 7–9 • Exam

Name _____ Period _____ Date _____

Answer each question and show all work clearly on a separate piece of paper.

1. Rewrite each equation in standard form and identify the type of curve.

    a. $x^2 - 14x - 3y + 43 = 0$ **b.** $16x^2 + 25y^2 - 64x - 336 = 0$

    c. $-11x^2 + 9y^2 + 44x + 90y + 82 = 0$ **d.** $x^2 + y^2 - 12x - 2y + 16 = 0$

2. Use $C = 3 + 2i$, $D = -7 + i$, and $E = 5 - 4i$ to evaluate each expression. Give answers in the form $a + bi$.

    a. $C + 2E$ **b.** $D \div E$ **c.** D^2 **d.** $CD + E$

3. Write an equation for a cubic function with real coefficients, zeros at 5 and $-3i$, and y-intercept -9.

4. Give the vertex and zeros of each quadratic function, and tell whether the vertex is a maximum or a minimum.

    a. $y = 5(x - 2)^2 + 7$ **b.** $y = -11(x + 9)(x + 2)$ **c.** $y = \frac{1}{4}x^2 - 2x + 4$

5. Find the value of x. Round answers to the nearest tenth.

    a.
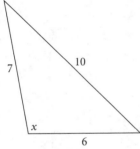
    b.
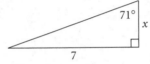
    c.
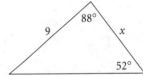

6. Port Byron is 120 miles directly north of Port Allen. Ship A leaves Port Allen, moving at a bearing of 60° and a speed of 21 mi/h. At the same time, ship B leaves Port Byron, moving at a bearing of 135° and a speed of 24 mi/h.

    a. Write parametric equations modeling the paths of the two ships. Assume that Port Allen is located at the origin and that due north is in the positive y-direction.

    b. After 4 hours, how far is ship A from Port Allen? How far is it from Port Byron?

    c. After 10 hours, how far apart are the two ships?

(continued)

Name _____ Period _____ Date _____

7. The motion of a ball thrown in the air is modeled with the parametric equations

$x = 93t \cos 25°$
$y = -16t^2 + 93t \sin 25° + 6$

   a. What are the initial velocity and angle of motion of the ball? From what height is the ball released?

   b. What is the position of the ball 1 second after it was released?

   c. How far does the ball travel? To the nearest hundredth of a second, when does it hit the ground?

8. Sketch a graph of each function. Include any asymptotes as dashed lines.

   a. $y = \dfrac{1}{(x + 3)^2}$ **b.** $y = \dfrac{x^2 + 4x + 3}{x + 3}$ **c.** $y = 3 + \dfrac{1}{x + 3}$

9. Perform each operation. Give your answers in factored form.

   a. $\dfrac{x - 3}{x^2 + x - 12} + \dfrac{2}{x^2 - 2x - 24}$

   b. $\dfrac{4x^2 + 20x + 24}{x^2 - x - 2} \cdot \dfrac{x^2 + 5x - 14}{2x^2 + 20x + 42}$

10. Write an equation in standard form for each conic section.

   a.

   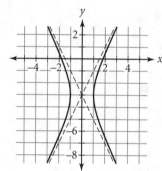

   b.

   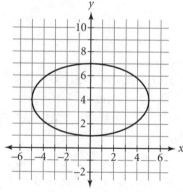

11. Write the equation $y = x^3 + 6x^2 - 25x - 150$ in factored form.

12. Solve this system of equations algebraically. Round the solutions to the nearest hundredth.

$$\begin{cases} x^2 + y^2 = 4 \\ y = 2x + 1 \end{cases}$$

Discovering Advanced Algebra Assessment Resources B
©2004 Key Curriculum Press

Chapter 10 • Quiz 1

Name _____ **Period** _____ **Date** _____

1. Find the exact value of the cosine or sine of each angle.

   a. $\sin(-150°)$ b. $\cos 135°$

2. Identify an angle θ with a measure between 0° and 360° that is coterminal with the given angle.

   a. $1160°$ b. $-747°$

3. Suppose $\cos \theta \approx 0.7547$. Find two possible values of θ in the domain $0° \leq \theta \leq 360°$.

4. Suppose $\sin \theta \approx 0.3090$. Find two possible values of θ in the domain $0° \leq \theta \leq 360°$.

5. Convert 320° to radians. Give the exact radian measure.

6. Convert $\frac{11\pi}{12}$ radians to degrees.

7. Find the exact length of arc AB.

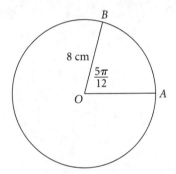

Chapter 10 • Quiz 2

Name _____ Period _____ Date _____

1. Write an equation for each sinusoid as a transformation of either
   $y = \sin x$ or $y = \cos x$.

   a.

   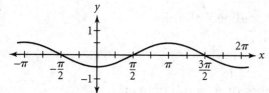

   b.

   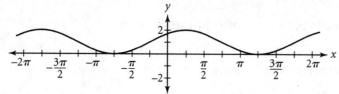

2. Find the principal value of $\sin^{-1}(-0.2588)$ to the nearest degree.

3. Find four values of x between -2π and 2π that satisfy $\cos x = \cos\frac{2\pi}{3}$.

4. Find the exact value of $\sin^{-1}(\sin 160°)$.

5. Consider the graph of the function

   $$y = 2.5 + 10\sin\left(\frac{2\pi(x - 25)}{15}\right)$$

   a. What is the vertical translation?

   b. What are the vertical stretch factor, minimum and maximum
      values, and amplitude?

   c. What are the horizontal stretch factor and period?

   d. What is the phase shift?

Discovering Advanced Algebra Assessment Resources B
©2004 Key Curriculum Press

Chapter 10 • Quiz 3

Name _____ Period _____ Date _____

1. Evaluate.

   a. $\cot\dfrac{\pi}{3}$

   b. $\csc\dfrac{11\pi}{6}$

   c. $\sec\pi$

2. Prove the identity

   $\cos A \cot A + \sin A = \csc A$

3. Prove the identity

   $\sin\left(\dfrac{\pi}{2} + A\right) = \cos A$

4. Rewrite the expression $\cos 13° \cos 47° - \sin 13° \sin 47°$ as a single sine or cosine, and then find its exact value.

5. Given $0 \leq x \leq \pi$ and $\sin x = \dfrac{3}{5}$, find the exact value of $\sin 2x$.

Chapter 10 • Test

Name _____ Period _____ Date _____

Answer each question and show all work clearly on a separate piece of paper.

1. Each number represents the measure of an angle in standard position. For each angle, tell which quadrant the angle's terminal side lies in, name a coterminal angle, and convert each angle measure from degrees to radians or vice versa.

    a. $300°$ b. $\dfrac{5\pi}{18}$ c. $165°$ d. $-\dfrac{7\pi}{8}$

2. Find the exact value of each expression.

    a. $\cos(-135°)$ b. $\sin\dfrac{5\pi}{3}$ c. $\sin 870°$ d. $\cos\dfrac{7\pi}{12}$

3. Consider the function $y = -1 + \cos 4(x - \pi)$.

    a. Identify the period, amplitude, phase shift, and vertical translation of the function.

    b. Sketch a graph of one complete cycle.

    c. Write the equation for another function that has the same graph.

4. Find the exact value of each expression.

    a. $\cos\left(\sin^{-1}\left(-\dfrac{8}{17}\right)\right)$ b. $\tan\left(\cos^{-1}\left(-\dfrac{5}{13}\right)\right)$ c. $\sin^{-1}\left(\sin\dfrac{4\pi}{3}\right)$

5. Identify the domain and range of $x = \sin y$ and $y = \sin^{-1} x$.

6. Write an equation for each graph.

    a.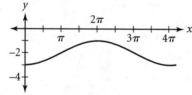

    b.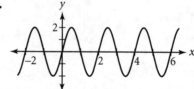

    c.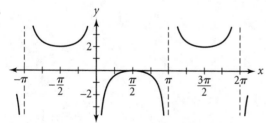

(continued)

Discovering Advanced Algebra Assessment Resources B
©2004 Key Curriculum Press

Name _____ **Period** _____ **Date** _____

7. Find the exact length of arc AB and the exact area of the shaded sector.

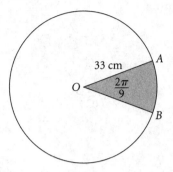

8. Prove each identity.

   a. $\cot^2 A = \dfrac{1 + \cos 2A}{1 - \cos 2A}$ **b.** $\tan\left(\dfrac{\pi}{2} - A\right) = \cot A$

9. Find the exact value of $\sin 72° \cos 27° - \cos 72° \sin 27°$.

10. Find all the solutions of $-7 + 3\cos(x - 5) = -6$ in the interval $0 \le x \le 2\pi$. Round solutions to the nearest hundredth.

Chapter 10 • Constructive Assessment Options

Choose one or more of these items to replace part of the chapter test. Let students know that they will receive from 0 to 5 points for each item, depending on the correctness and completeness of their answer.

1. *(Lessons 10.1–10.3, 10.5)*
   The period T of a pendulum can be calculated by using the formula

   $$T = 2\pi\sqrt{\frac{l}{g}}$$

   where l is the length of the pendulum in meters and g is the acceleration due to gravity (9.8 m/s²). In this pendulum, the bob is suspended on a 4 m cable and swings through an angle of 0.77 radian. A motion sensor is set up 0.5 m from the starting point of the pendulum's swing.

   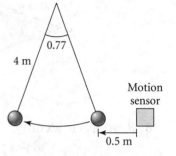

   a. What is the length of the arc along which the pendulum bob moves?

   b. What is the maximum distance of the bob from the motion sensor? Explain how you found your answer.

   c. You can write a trigonometric equation to model the horizontal distance of the bob from the motion sensor as a function of time. (Assume that the bob travels on a straight line.) What is the period of the function? What is the amplitude? Explain how you found your answers.

   d. Write an equation for the distance, d, of the bob from the motion sensor as a function of time, t.

   e. How far will the bob be from the sensor at 6.2 s?

   f. Find the first four times when the bob is 1.3 m from the sensor.

2. *(Lessons 10.2, 10.4, 10.6)*
   Consider the function $y = 2\cos^2 x - 2\sin x - 2.3$.

   a. Graph the function for $-4\pi \le x \le 4\pi$.

   b. Is the function periodic? If so, what is its period?

   c. Graphically estimate all the zeros of the function between 0 and 2π to the nearest tenth of a radian.

   d. Write the function in a form that includes only one type of trigonometric function. Show and explain your work.

   e. Algebraically, find all the zeros of the functions between 0 and 2π to the nearest thousandth of a radian. Show and explain your work.

3. *(Lessons 10.6, 10.7)*
   Find the exact trigonometric values for each angle. Show each step. Express your answers with rational denominators.

   a. $\sin 15°$
   b. $\cot 105°$
   c. $\csc 255°$

   (continued)

Discovering Advanced Algebra Assessment Resources B
©2004 Key Curriculum Press

4. *(Lessons 10.1– 10.3, 10.5, 10.7)*

Sandra decides to ride the inclined ferris wheel at the LotsaFun Amusement Park. The ferris wheel has a 7-foot radius and is supported at its center by an inclined cable. The cable forms an angle of 30° with the ground. The wheel turns clockwise as it moves up the cable. Its center moves at a speed of 5 ft/s along the cable, and it completes one revolution every 10 seconds. The seats are located along the circumference of the wheel. When the wheel starts moving, Sandra's seat is at ground level. Express all angle measures in radians.

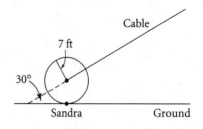

a. Write an equation that describes the height of the wheel's center above the ground as a function of time. Explain how you found your answer. Graph the equation, showing the first 30 seconds.

b. Write an equation that describes Sandra's height with respect to the center of the wheel as a function of time. Explain how you found your answer. Graph the equation, showing the first 30 seconds.

c. Find an equation that models Sandra's height with respect to the ground as a function of time. Graph the equation, showing the first 30 seconds.

d. After 30 seconds, the ride stops. How far is Sandra from the ground?

e. At what time during the first 30 seconds is Sandra at the maximum height? What is the maximum height? Give your answers to the nearest tenth.

f. Use parametric equations to model Sandra's movement. Graph the equations and describe the ride. (By the way, the ride reverses direction, and Sandra gets back to the ground the same way she got up.)

Chapter 11 • Quiz 1

Name _____ Period _____ Date _____

1. Write $\displaystyle\sum_{n=1}^{4} \left(3n^2 - 12\right)$ as a sum of terms, and then calculate the sum.

2. Find the sum of the first 40 multiples of 6: $\left\{6, 12, 18, 24, \ldots, u_{40}\right\}$.

3. Find $\displaystyle\sum_{n=25}^{50} (3n - 2)$.

4. Kelly did 18 sit-ups on January 1. For the rest of the month, she increased the number of sit-ups she did by 6 each day.

   a. How many sit-ups did Kelly do on January 31?

   b. How many sit-ups did Kelly do altogether during the month of January?

Chapter 11 • Quiz 2

Name _____ Period _____ Date _____

1. Find the indicated sum.

   a. $\sum\limits_{n=1}^{\infty} 16(0.6)^n$ **b.** $\sum\limits_{n=1}^{7} 8(1.25)^{n-1}$

   c. $20 + 10 + 5 + \cdots + 0.078125$ **d.** $\sum\limits_{n=15}^{30} 160(0.85)^{n-1}$

   e. $\sum\limits_{n=5}^{\infty} 24(0.7)^{n-1}$

2. In the pattern below, the side lengths of each rectangle are $\frac{2}{3}$ the side lengths of the previous rectangle.

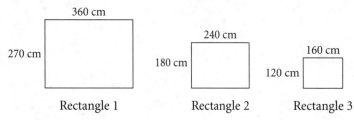

a. If this pattern were continued forever, what would be the sum of the perimeters?

b. If this pattern were continued forever, what would be the sum of the areas?

Discovering Advanced Algebra Assessment Resources B
©2004 Key Curriculum Press

Chapter 11 • Test

Name _____ Period _____ Date _____

Answer each question and show all work clearly on a separate piece of paper.

1. Consider the sequence

   5, 11, 17, 23, 29, 35, . . .

   a. What is the 92nd term?

   b. Which term has value 215?

   c. Find S_{38}.

   d. Find the sum of all the terms with values between 100 and 200.

2. Consider the sequence

   500, 400, 320, 256, . . .

   a. Find u_{25}.

   b. Find S_{25}.

   c. Find the sum of all the terms with values greater than 20.

   d. Find the sum $500 + 400 + 320 + 256 + \cdots$.

3. Express the infinite series below using sigma (Σ) notation, and then find the sum.

   $128 + 80 + 50 + 31.25 + \cdots$

4. Yolanda begins a job with a starting salary of $25,000. She is guaranteed a raise of 5.25% each year. Carlos also starts a job with a salary of $25,000. He is guaranteed a raise of $1,500 each year.

   a. What will be Yolanda's salary the fifth year? What total amount will she have earned in five years?

   b. What will be Carlos's salary the fifth year? What total amount will he have earned in five years?

   c. Suppose Yolanda and Carlos keep their jobs for 25 years. Who will have earned the greater total amount over the 25-year period? How much more money will that person have earned?

5. Find the indicated sum.

   a. $\displaystyle\sum_{n=1}^{20} (3n - 17)$

   b. $\displaystyle\sum_{n=1}^{\infty} 25\left(\frac{5}{9}\right)^{n-1}$

   c. $\displaystyle\sum_{n=13}^{31} (2n + 6)$

   d. $\displaystyle\sum_{n=15}^{\infty} 450(0.85)^{n-1}$

   e. $\displaystyle\sum_{n=24}^{36} 12(1.12)^{n-1}$

(continued)

Name _____ Period _____ Date _____

6. Consider this sequence of toothpick figures.

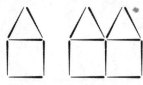 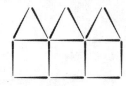 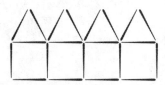

Figure 1   Figure 2   Figure 3   Figure 4

  a. If this pattern continues, how many toothpicks will be in Figure 15?

  b. What total number of toothpicks would be needed to build Figures 1 through 40?

7. An ideal ball is dropped from an initial height of 64 cm and bounces on its own. The rebound heights to the nearest centimeter are 48, 36, 27, 20, and so on. What is the total distance the ball will travel, both up and down, in infinitely many bounces?

8. Find the sum of the multiples of 8 from 80 to 480.

Discovering Advanced Algebra Assessment Resources B
©2004 Key Curriculum Press

Chapter 11 • Constructive Assessment Options

Choose one or more of these items to replace part of the chapter test. Let students know that they will receive from 0 to 5 points for each item, depending on the correctness and completeness of their answer.

1. *(Lesson 11.1)*
This table shows music CD sales during the 1990s.

a. Plot the data on a scatter plot, and model the data with an appropriate equation. Explain how you chose your equation.

b. Use your model to estimate the total sales for 1991 through 2000. Show and explain your work.

c. If the trend continues, what will be the total expenditure for the current decade (2001 through 2010)? Do you think your prediction is reasonable? Explain.

Year	CD sales ($ millions)
1991	4,338
1993	6,511
1995	9,377
1997	9,915
1999	12,816

(The World Almanac and Book of Facts 2002)

2. *(Lesson 11.1)*
Using series, you can find shortcuts for adding odd or even numbers.

a. Write an expression for the sum of the first 35 odd numbers using sigma (Σ) notation.

b. What is the sum of the first 35 odd numbers?

c. What is the sum of the first 12 odd numbers? Of the first 8 odd numbers? Of the first 20 odd numbers?

d. Based on your answers to parts b and c, come up with a shortcut for finding the sum of the first k odd numbers. Use your shortcut to find the sum of the first 68 odd numbers.

e. Find the sum of the odd numbers between 150 and 324. Explain how you found your answer.

f. Use sigma notation to write an expression for the sum of the first p even numbers.

g. Use the formula for the partial sum of a series to find the sum of the first p even numbers. Explain how you found your answer.

h. What is the sum of the first 26 even numbers?

i. What is the sum of the even numbers between 81 and 123? Explain how you found your answer.

(continued)

3. *(Lessons 11.2, 11.3)*

The figures below are the first four stages in the creation of a fractal. The side length of the square in Stage 0 is 6 cm. At each subsequent stage, a square is added to the middle third of each edge of each square from the previous stage, as shown.

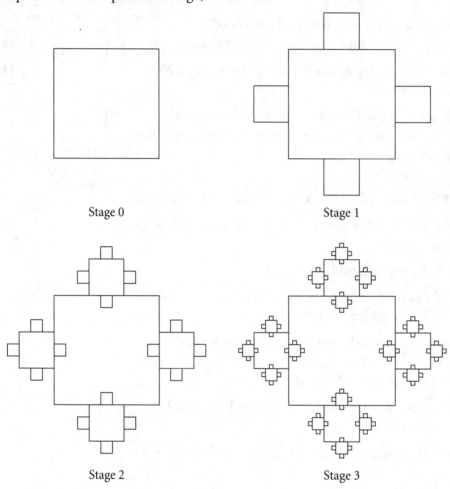

Stage 0   Stage 1

Stage 2   Stage 3

a. Consider the areas of the squares. Show all your work.

   i. What is the sum of the areas of all the squares in Stage 3, including overlapping areas?

   ii. What will be the sum of the areas of the squares in Stage 7?

   iii. If the fractal continues indefinitely, what will be the sum of the areas?

b. Now consider only the "new" area at each stage. In other words, do not count the overlapping area. Show all your work.

   i. What is the area of Stage 3?

   ii. What will be the area of Stage 7?

   iii. What will be the area of the fractal after infinitely many stages?

c. What is the eventual outside perimeter of the fractal? Explain how you found your answer.

(continued)

4. *(Lessons 11.2, 11.3)*

The Olsons are considering joining a club. They have a choice of two membership plans.

Plan A: Pay $125 the first year; each subsequent year, pay $125 more than you paid the previous year.

Plan B: Pay $1000 the first year; each subsequent year, pay two-thirds what you paid the previous year.

a. For each plan, write a formula for S_n, the total amount paid over the first n years. Show and explain how you found your formula.

b. Set your calculator to Function mode, and graph the two formulas from part a in the same window. When is each plan the "better deal"? Explain how you found your answer.

c. Describe at least two factors that the Olsons should consider when choosing a plan.

Chapter 12 • Quiz 1

Name _____ Period _____ Date _____

1. This table gives information about how students at South High get to school each morning. Assume that the table accounts for every student in the school. Express each answer to the nearest .001.

	Bus	Car	Walk	Bike	Total
10th grade	256	48	103	74	481
11th grade	210	94	72	90	466
12th grade	146	168	84	43	441
Total	612	310	259	207	1388

   a. What is the probability that a randomly chosen student takes the bus to school?

   b. What is the probability that a randomly chosen bike rider is in 12th grade?

   c. What is the probability that a randomly chosen 11th grader walks to school?

2. If you randomly select one number between 0 and 4 and one number between 4 and 7, what is the probability that the sum of the numbers will be greater than or equal to 8?

3. A bag contains four red blocks, eight blue blocks, and two yellow blocks.

   a. Suppose you draw a block at random, return it to the bag, and then draw another block. What is the probability that you will get two red blocks in a row?

   b. Suppose you draw a block at random, *do not* return it to the bag, and then draw another block. What is the probability that you will get two red blocks in a row?

4. The probability that a randomly selected student at Simon's school has a dog is .38; the probability that the student has a cat and a dog is .12; and the probability that the student has neither a cat nor a dog is .40. What is the probability that the student has a cat?

Chapter 12 • Quiz 2

Name _____ Period _____ Date _____

1. Zina has an 80% free-throw shooting percentage. She is at the foul line and is in a one-and-one free-throw situation. (This means that if she scores on her first shot, she gets to take a second shot. If she misses on her first shot, she does not get to take a second shot.)

   a. Find the probability that Zina will get 0 points, the probability that she will get 1 point, and the probability that she will get 2 points. (*Note:* She gets 1 point for each shot she makes.)

   b. What is Zina's expected value in a one-and-one situation?

2. Students who use the computer lab are randomly assigned a four-character password consisting of a letter, followed by two digits between 0 and 9, followed by one digit between 0 and 4.

   a. How many different passwords are possible?

   b. What is the probability that Rashid's password will start with a vowel (A, E, I, O, or U) and have three odd digits?

3. Megan has six framed photographs from her trip to Ireland. She wants to put three of them in a horizontal row on her bedroom wall.

   a. How many different arrangements are possible?

   b. If Megan chooses the photographs and ordering at random, what is the probability that her favorite photograph, which shows the island of Skellig Michael, will be first in the horizontal row?

Chapter 12 • Quiz 3

Name _____ Period _____ Date _____

1. Luigi's Pizzeria offers 12 different pizza toppings, including pepperoni, garlic, pineapple, and black olives.

   a. How many different three-topping pizzas are possible?

   b. How many different four-topping pizzas are possible?

   c. How many of the possible four-topping pizzas do not include pepperoni or black olives?

   d. Stella decides to live dangerously. She tells Luigi to choose four toppings at random to put on her pizza. What is the probability that Stella's pizza will include both pineapple and garlic?

2. Find the 1st term and the 8th term in the expansion of $(a + b)^{14}$.

3. Suppose you roll four dice. Find the probabilities that you will get 0, 1, 2, 3, and 4 twos. Give the probabilities to the nearest .0001.

Chapter 12 • Test

Name _____ Period _____ Date _____

Answer each question and show all work clearly on a separate piece
of paper.

1. Consider the diagram at right.

   a. What is the probability that a randomly plotted point will be in
the white region in the lower left corner? Give your answer to
the nearest .001.

   b. If 720 points are plotted at random, about how many of them
would you expect to be in the shaded region?

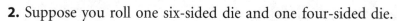

2. Suppose you roll one six-sided die and one four-sided die.

   a. What is the probability that you will get a sum less than 4?

   b. What is the probability that you will get a sum greater than 5?

   c. What is the expected value of the sum?

3. An ice cream store has 12 ice cream flavors.

   a. Chuck wants a sugar cone with three scoops of ice cream in
different flavors. If the order of the scoops matters to Chuck—for
example, if he considers having a scoop of chocolate on the top as
different from having a scoop of chocolate in the middle or on
the bottom—how many different possibilities does he have to
choose from?

   b. The store makes its hot fudge sundaes using three scoops of ice
cream. How many different three-scoop combinations are possible?
(Assume that two or even all three scoops may be the same flavor.)

   c. The store sells four kinds of ice cream cones and three kinds of
sprinkles. If Zelda wants a cone with one scoop of ice cream and
one type of sprinkle, how many different possibilities does she
have to choose from?

4. Find the indicated term of the binomial expansion.

   a. The 1st term of $(2 + z)^9$

   b. The 6th term of $\left(1 + \frac{z}{2}\right)^{12}$

   c. The 19th term of $(p + q)^{20}$

(continued)

Discovering Advanced Algebra Assessment Resources B
©2004 Key Curriculum Press

Name_____ Period_____ Date_____

5. A deck of cards contains 13 cards of each suit (clubs, spades, hearts, and diamonds).

   a. Suppose you draw a card at random, put the card back in the deck, shuffle the cards, and then draw another card. What is the probability that you will draw two hearts?

   b. Suppose you draw two cards at random without replacing the first card before drawing the second. What is the probability that you will draw two hearts?

   c. Suppose you draw four cards at random without replacing any of the cards. What is the probability that you will get one card of each suit?

6. Theo is participating in a free-throw competition. To advance to the second round, he must make at least 12 of 15 free throws. If Theo's free-throw shooting percentage is 76%, what is the probability that he will advance to the next round? Round your answer to the nearest .001.

7. The following statements describe the books on Pete's bookshelf:

   i. 62% do not have illustrations.

   ii. None of the novels have illustrations.

   iii. 73% are novels or have illustrations.

   iv. 6% are paperbacks with illustrations.

   v. 10% are novels that are not paperbacks.

   vi. 15% are not paperbacks, are not novels, and do not have illustrations.

A book is selected at random from the shelf. Let K represent the event that the book is a paperback, let N represent the event that the book is a novel, and let I represent the event that the book has illustrations.

   a. Description i can be rewritten as the probability statement $P(\text{not } I) = .62$. Translate the other descriptions into probability statements.

   b. Create a Venn diagram showing all the probabilities in this situation.

Chapter 12 • Constructive Assessment Options

Choose one or more of these items to replace part of the chapter test. Let students know that they will receive from 0 to 5 points for each item, depending on the correctness and completeness of their answer.

1. *(Lessons 12.1–12.3)*

A, B, C, and D are independent events. $P(A) = .7$, $P(B) = .6$, $P(C) = .5$, and $P(D) = .4$. Cut out four circles to represent the probabilities of the four events.

a. Place the $P(A)$ circle and the $P(B)$ circle on the table so that they overlap but do not coincide.

   i. Use your model to explain why $P(A \text{ or } B)$ equals $P(A) + P(B) - P(A \text{ and } B)$.

   ii. Find $P(A \text{ or } B)$, $P(A \text{ or } C)$, and $P(C \text{ or } D)$. Show your work.

b. Place the circles for $P(A)$, $P(B)$, and $P(C)$ on the table so that they all overlap but none coincide. Make a sketch of your model.

   i. Use your model to find and explain a rule for computing $P(A \text{ or } B \text{ or } C)$.

   ii. Find $P(A \text{ or } B \text{ or } C)$, $P(A \text{ or } C \text{ or } D)$, and $P(B \text{ or } C \text{ or } D)$.

c. Place all four circles on the table so that they all overlap but none coincide. (At least one of the circles will have to be an oval.)

   i. Find a rule for computing $P(A \text{ or } B \text{ or } C \text{ or } D)$.

   ii. Find $P(A \text{ or } B \text{ or } C \text{ or } D)$.

d. Use your results from parts a–c to complete parts i–iii.

   i. Find $P(\text{not } A)$, $P(\text{not } B)$, $P(\text{not } C)$, and $P(\text{not } D)$.

   ii. Find $P(\text{not } A \text{ and not } B \text{ and not } C \text{ and not } D)$.

   iii. Explain the relationship between the answers to parts cii and dii.

(continued)

Discovering Advanced Algebra Assessment Resources B
©2004 Key Curriculum Press

2. *(Lessons 12.1, 12.2, 12.4)*
Consider a standard deck of 52 cards.

a. What is the probability of drawing three cards at random from the deck and not getting a pair? Show your calculation.

b. To play the game Match, you randomly turn over up to four cards, one at a time. You win as soon as you get a pair. If you turn over four cards and don't get a pair, you lose. Construct a tree diagram to help you complete parts i–iv.

  i. Find P(2-card win), the probability of winning with two cards.

  ii. Find P(3-card win), the probability of winning with exactly three cards.

  iii. Find P(4-card win).

  iv. What is the probability of not winning in four cards?

c. In Match, you receive 10 points for winning with two cards, 8 points for winning with three cards, and 6 points for winning with four cards. If you do not win in four cards, you lose 3 points. What is your expected score after 10 games of Match? Explain.

d. Match can be modified by changing the number of cards a player turns over. What is the least number of cards that would have to be turned over to make the probability of winning greater than the probability of losing? Explain.

3. *(Lessons 12.1, 12.5, 12.6)*
Use combinations and permutations to complete parts a–c. Explain each answer.

a. Robert's favorite shirt has seven buttons. Every time he wears it, he fastens the buttons in a different order (always matching a button with its correct hole). If he wears the shirt twice a week, how long will it take him to go through every possible sequence of buttons?

b. Ashton, Bart, and Carlos are among 11 students who volunteer to participate in a school study. Participants are called in a random order. What is the probability that the three boys will be called one immediately after the other?

c. Sandy, Aisha, and 10 other girls play baseball. Only 9 girls can be on the field at a time. (Assume that any girl can play any position.)

  i. How many different teams of 9 girls can be formed?

  ii. Consider two teams to be different if any player is in a new position. How many different teams can be formed?

  iii. If a team is randomly selected from among the 12 girls, what is the probability that both Sandy and Aisha will be on the team?

  iv. What is the probability that Aisha will be the pitcher and Sandy will not be on the team?

(continued)

4. (*Lessons 12.1–12.3, 12.6, 12.7*)

The Cabot High girl's basketball team has only five players. The table shows shooting statistics for the team. (*Note:* The shooting frequency is the percentage of all the team's shots taken by the player.) In parts a–h, show your calculations.

Player	Shooting success	Shooting frequency
Shauna	62%	24%
Tia	72%	18%
Bebe	48%	6%
Marie	81%	40%
Noriko	54%	12%

a. What is the probability that the next shot will be taken by Marie and will be good?

b. What is the team's shooting success?

c. The team just won a game by a score of 73 to 58. If everyone performed as expected, how many points did Marie score?

d. What is the probability that the sequence for the next two shots will be Marie misses and then Noriko scores?

e. Assuming that each girl makes one shot, what is the probability that all the girls will score on their next shots?

f. What is the probability that Shauna will make at least two out of her next three shots?

g. What is the probability that Noriko will make at most two out of her next four shots?

h. What is the probability that if Shauna, Tia, and Marie each take one shot, at least one shot will be good?

Chapter 13 • Quiz 1

Name _____ Period _____ Date _____

1. A random-number generator selects a number, x, according to the probability distribution below.

   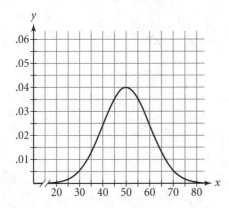

   a. Find $P(x = 5)$. **b.** Find $P(x < 7)$.

   c. Find $P(3 < x < 7)$. **d.** Find the mode and median of the distribution.

2. Estimate the mean and standard deviation of the normal distribution represented by this graph.

   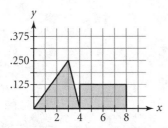

3. A filling machine fills jars with 17.85 ounces of peanut butter, with a standard deviation of 0.3 ounce. The label on the jars claims that the weight of the peanut butter is 18 ounces.

   a. What is the probability that a randomly selected jar will contain between 17.5 and 18 ounces of peanut butter?

   b. What percentage of the jars filled actually contain 18 ounces or more of peanut butter?

Chapter 13 • Quiz 2

Name _____ Period _____ Date _____

1. A set of normally distributed data values has a mean of 120 and a standard deviation of 6.4.

   a. Find the z-value that corresponds to a data value of 112.

   b. Find the data value that corresponds to a z-value of 1.4.

2. A sample of 40 data values is taken from a normally distributed population. The mean of the sample is 117 and the standard deviation is 13. Find the 68% and 95% confidence intervals.

3. A population has a mean of 325 and a standard deviation of 24. If a sample of size 64 is randomly selected from the population, what is the probability that the sample will have a mean of 320 or less?

4. The label on each box of Super Sesame Snacks states that the weight of the contents is 36 ounces. A consumer magazine analyzes 40 boxes and finds that the mean weight is 34.7 ounces, with a standard deviation of 4.2 ounces. If the label is correct, what is the probability that a 40-box sample will have a mean weight of 34.7 ounces or less?

Discovering Advanced Algebra Assessment Resources B
©2004 Key Curriculum Press

Chapter 13 • Quiz 3

Name _____ Period _____ Date _____

1. Tell which of the following correlation coefficients best describes each data set: $-.90$, $-.56$, $.09$, or $.85$.

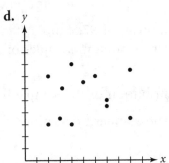

2. This table shows the number of twin births in the United States from 1990 to 2000.

   a. Find the equation of the least squares line for these data. Use 1990 as the reference year. (That is, let x represent the number of years after 1990.)

   b. Find the root mean square error for the least squares model.

   c. Use the model to predict the number of twin births in 1991. How does your prediction compare to the actual value of 94.8 thousand?

Year	Twin births (thousands)	Year	Twin births (thousands)
1990	93.9	1996	100.8
1992	95.4	1997	104.1
1993	96.4	1998	110.7
1994	97.1	1999	114.3
1995	96.7	2000	118.9

(*The World Almanac and Book of Facts 2002* and *www.infoplease.com*)

3. Consider these data.

x	1	2	3	4	5	6
y	1	5	8	17	25	41

   a. Find quadratic and cubic models for these data.

   b. Find the root mean square error for each model you found in part a.

Chapter 13 • Test

Name _____ Period _____ Date _____

Answer each question and show all work clearly on a separate piece of paper.

1. Consider this probability distribution of a random variable, *x*.

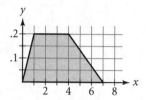

a. Find the median of the distribution.

b. Find $P(2.5 < x < 7)$.

c. Find $P(x < 2.5)$.

d. Find $P(x = 3)$.

2. A skewed-right population has a mean of 97.5 and a standard deviation of 11.9. A large number of random samples of size 36 are taken from the population.

a. Describe the shape of the distribution of the sample means.

b. Give the approximate mean and standard deviation of the sample means.

3. This table shows the median price of single-family homes in randomly selected areas in 1999 and 2000.

Metropolitan area	1999 price ($ thousands)	2000 price ($ thousands)
Reno, NV	150.6	157.3
Kalamazoo, MI	110.9	109.9
Jackson, MS	95.1	99.5
Lake County, IL	164.0	169.4
New York metropolitan area, NY/NJ/CT	203.2	230.2
Providence, RI	128.8	137.8
Cedar Rapids, IA	105.8	112.9
Lansing/East Lansing, MI	105.2	111.2
Eugene/Springfield, OR	129.5	132.8
Nashville, TN	116.4	147.5
Greenville/Spartanburg, SC	113.8	118.1
Raleigh/Durham, NC	165.0	158.4

(*The World Almanac and Book of Facts 2002*)

(continued)

Discovering Advanced Algebra Assessment Resources B
©2004 Key Curriculum Press

    a. Make a scatter plot of these data. Does there appear to be a linear relationship between the 1999 and 2000 prices? Use the correlation coefficient to justify your answer.

    b. Find the equation of the least squares line that models these data. (Round the coefficient and constant to the nearest hundredth.) Give the real-world meaning of the slope and *y*-intercept of the line.

    c. Find the root mean square error for the least squares model.

    d. The 1999 median price for a home in Milwaukee, Wisconsin, was $135,300. Use your equation to predict the 2000 median price for a home in Milwaukee.

4. All the geometry classes at Lincoln High took the same final exam. The scores were normally distributed with a mean of 70.4 and a standard deviation of 9.6.

    a. What is the probability that a randomly selected geometry student received a score between 75 and 80?

    b. What is the probability that a randomly selected geometry student received a score less than 65?

    c. What is the probability that a randomly selected geometry student received a score greater than 90?

    d. The mean score for the 16 students in Ms. Ito's fifth-period honors geometry class was 77. How likely would it be for a *randomly selected* sample of 16 geometry students to have a mean score of 77 or more?

5. The transit authority in a major city claims that it takes an average of 30 minutes to travel by subway from a particular suburban stop to a stop in the downtown area. Tim travels this route to work every day. He times his commute for 25 days and finds that the mean travel time is 35 minutes, with a standard deviation of 12 minutes. Based on Tim's results, do you think the transit authority's claim is accurate? Justify your answer.

6. Based on a sample, the 95% confidence interval for the mileage of a particular gas-electric "hybrid" car is between 42.34 and 49.66 mi/gal. What is the 68% confidence interval?

    (continued)

7. This table shows the number of cable TV systems in the United States each year from 1983 to 2000.

Year	Number of cable systems	Year	Number of cable systems
1983	5,600	1992	11,073
1984	6,200	1993	11,108
1985	6,600	1994	11,214
1986	7,500	1995	11,215
1987	7,900	1996	11,220
1988	8,500	1997	10,943
1989	9,050	1998	10,845
1990	9,575	1999	10,700
1991	10,704	2000	10,500

(*The World Almanac and Book of Facts 2002*)

a. Find the equation of a quadratic model for these data, using 1980 as year 0. (So, for example, $x = 3$ represents 1983, $x = 4$ represents 1984, and so on.)

b. Find the equation of a cubic model for these data, using 1980 as year 0.

c. Plot the data and the equations for both models. Which model appears to be a better fit?

d. Find the root mean square error for each model. Based on your results, which model is a better fit?

e. Using the model that is the better fit, predict the number of cable systems in 2001. (The actual number of cable systems in 2001 was 10,929.)

f. Using the model that is the better fit, predict the first year there will be fewer than 2000 cable systems.

Chapter 13 • Constructive Assessment Options

Choose one or more of these items to replace part of the chapter test. Let students know that they will receive from 0 to 5 points for each item, depending on the correctness and completeness of their answer.

1. *(Lessons 13.5–13.7)*

   The table below gives consumer price indexes (CPIs) for food and beverages and for medical care from 1970 to 2000. The CPIs show how prices in a given year compare with prices in the period from 1982 to 1984, which have a CPI of 100. For example, in 1990, prices for food and beverages were 32.1% higher than they were during 1982 to 1984.

Year	1970	1975	1980	1985	1990	1995	1998	1999	2000
Food/beverage CPI	40.1	60.2	86.7	105.6	132.1	148.9	161.1	164.6	168.4
Medical CPI	34.0	47.5	74.9	113.5	162.8	220.5	242.1	250.6	260.8

   (*The World Almanac and Book of Facts 2002*)

   a. Find the correlation coefficient for the relationship between the year, x, and the food and beverage CPI, y. Use 1960 as year 0.

   b. Find the correlation coefficient for the relationship between the year, x, and the medical care CPI, y. Use 1960 as year 0.

   c. Compare the correlation coefficients in parts a and b.

   d. In the early 1970s, medical care costs rose more slowly than food and beverage costs; but more recently, they have increased more quickly. So the relationship between year and medical care CPI may not be linear. Find the correlation coefficient between *year* and log(*medical CPI*) and between log(*year*) and log(*medical CPI*).

   e. Use the best correlation you found in part d to write an equation to model the rising medical care CPI. Show your work.

   f. Plot the (*year, medical CPI*) data and your equation from part e. Find the root mean square error of your model.

   (continued)

2. *(Lessons 13.2–13.4)*

Alison rides her bike to and from school every day. She has been keeping track of her travel times. Her home-to-school times are normally distributed with mean 16 min 15 s and standard deviation 2 min 30 s. Her school-to-home times are normally distributed with mean 20 min 40 s and standard deviation 6 min.

a. Plot the normal distributions for both the home-to-school times and school-to-home times on the same screen. Describe some possible reasons for the differences in the two curves.

b. Find the *z*-values for trips to or from school that take 18 min.

c. What is the probability that it will take Alison more than 18 min to get to school? More than 18 min to get home?

d. About how often does it take Alison more than 30 min to get home?

e. About how often does Alison make a trip to or from school in less than 15 min? Explain your reasoning.

f. When Alison makes her very fastest trips, is she generally going to school or coming home? Explain how you know.

3. *(Lessons 13.5, 13.6)*

Eric is comparing domestic animals with wild animals. He has collected these data. Complete parts a–d for each group of animals.

Domestic Animals

Animal	Gestation period (days)	Longevity (years)
Cat	63	12
Dog	61	12
Guinea pig	68	4
Horse	330	20
Pig	112	10
Rabbit	31	5
Sheep	154	12

Wild Animals

Animal	Gestation period (days)	Longevity (years)
Beaver	105	5
Chipmunk	31	6
African elephant	660	35
Kangaroo	36	7
Lion	100	15
Moose	240	12
Zebra	365	15

(*The World Almanac and Book of Facts 2000*)

a. Find the mean and standard deviation of both variables.

b. Find the correlation coefficient between the variables.

c. Find the least squares line and the root mean square error.

d. Find the median-median line and its root mean square error.

e. Discuss the accuracy of the four models you found. Which model would you use to predict the longevity of domestic animals? Of wild animals? Use statistics to support your answers.

Chapters 10–13 • Exam

Name _____   Period _____   Date _____

Answer each question and show all work clearly on a separate piece of paper.

1. Find the exact value of each expression.

   a. $\cos 240°$

   b. $\csc\left(-\dfrac{5\pi}{4}\right)$

   c. $\cot\dfrac{2\pi}{3}$

   d. $\cos(75°)$

   e. $\tan\left(\sin^{-1}\left(-\dfrac{8}{17}\right)\right)$

   f. $\cos^{-1}(\cos 295°)$

2. Reyna is taking a college entrance exam in 17 days. To prepare for the vocabulary section, she plans to learn 4 new words tonight, 8 words tomorrow, 12 words the next night, and so on, each night increasing the number of new words by 4. If she sticks to her plan, how many new words will she have to learn the 16th night (the night before the test)? What total number of new words will she have learned in the 16 nights before the test?

3. Circle P has diameter 18 inches. Find the length of arc AB and the area of the shaded sector.

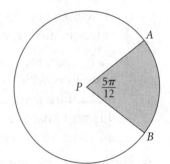

4. Find the indicated sum.

   a. $\displaystyle\sum_{n=11}^{32}(2.5n - 7)$

   b. $\displaystyle\sum_{n=1}^{\infty}275\left(\dfrac{1}{5}\right)^{n-1}$

   c. $\displaystyle\sum_{n=1}^{22}1.4(1.65)^{n-1}$

5. A frozen yogurt company claims that a serving of their strawberry frozen yogurt has only 60 calories. A consumer group analyzes 30 samples (taken from different cartons and different locations) and finds these calorie counts.

   58 58 65 58 69 67 58 62 60 59

   63 65 58 61 59 65 62 60 57 63

   61 65 67 59 63 58 60 63 64 59

   Based on these results, do you think the company's claim is accurate? Explain your reasoning.

6. From past experience, Zora knows that the probability that she will beat her older sister at a basketball video game is .70, and the probability that she will beat her sister in a real one-on-one basketball game is .25. The sisters plan to challenge each other at video basketball this morning and real basketball this afternoon.

   a. What is the probability that Zora will win both games?

   b. What is the probability that Zora will win at least one game?

   c. What is the probability that Zora will win exactly one game?

(continued)

Name _____ Period _____ Date _____

7. Write an equation for each graph.

a.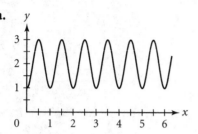

b.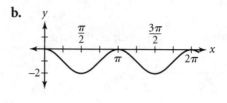

8. Customers at an Internet store must choose a four-character password when they set up their accounts. The characters in a password can be letters or numbers.

  a. How many different passwords are possible?

  b. How many of the possible passwords have one number followed by three letters?

  c. How many of the possible passwords have one number and three letters in any order?

  d. Each week, the store chooses a password at random and awards customers with that password a $100 gift certificate. What is the probability that the password chosen this week will have four different characters? What is the probability that it will have four different numbers?

9. Simon is competing in an archery competition. In the third round of the competition, each player shoots four arrows. A player receives 10 points for each arrow that hits the bull's-eye. No points are awarded for arrows that miss the bull's-eye. From past experience, Simon knows he has a 78% chance of hitting the bull's-eye on any one shot.

  a. Find the probabilities that Simon will get 0, 1, 2, 3, and 4 bull's-eyes.

  b. What is Simon's expected value for the third round?

10. Consider the data at right. In parts b–d, round your answers to thousandths.

  a. Find the correlation coefficient for these data.

  b. Find the equation for the least squares line for these data.

  c. Find an equation for a power model for these data.

  d. Find an equation for an exponential model for these data.

  e. Find the root mean square error for each model you found in parts b–d. Based on your results, which model fits the data best?

x	y
1	1.7
2	3.1
3	4.0
4	4.6
5	5.8
6	6.5
7	7.4

Discovering Advanced Algebra Assessment Resources B
©2004 Key Curriculum Press

Final Exam

Name _____ Period _____ Date _____

Answer each question and show all work clearly on a separate piece of paper.

1. Consider the sequence

15625, 9375, 5625, 3375, 2025, . . .

   a. Write a recursive rule for the sequence. Call the first term u_1.

   b. Write an explicit formula for the nth term of the sequence.

   c. What is u_{10}?

   d. What is the sum of the first ten terms?

   e. What is the sum of all the terms?

2. Three basketball players are practicing free throws at different baskets in the gym. Arlene makes 80% of her shots, Bethany makes 56% of her shots, and Carlotta makes 72% of her shots. Draw a tree diagram to represent all of the possible outcomes for the three free-throw shooters. Then find each probability described.

   a. The probability that all three will be successful

   b. The probability that Bethany will make her shot but Arlene and Carlotta will miss their shots

   c. The probability that exactly two players will make their shots

   d. The probability that at least two players will make their shots

3. Sketch a graph of each equation.

   a. $\left(\dfrac{x}{3}\right)^2 + \left(\dfrac{y+1}{2}\right)^2 = 1$ **b.** $\dfrac{y-1}{3} = (x-2)^2$

   c. $-x^2 + 2x + 2y^2 + 8y + 5 = 0$

4. For each equation in Problem 3, identify the vertices, foci, and directrix, where applicable.

5. Write the function $f(x) = x^4 - \frac{5}{2}x^3 + 10x^2 - \frac{45}{2}x + 9$ in factored form.

6. For two months, a veterinarian counts the number of kittens in each new litter born. He gathers these data.

     {1, 4, 5, 4, 1, 3, 2, 5, 2, 4, 3, 1, 6, 4, 6, 4, 5}

   a. What are the mean, median, and mode of the data?

   b. Draw a box plot of the data. Describe the shape of the data.

   c. What is the standard deviation of the data?

   d. 68% of births should result in a number of kittens in what range?

(continued)

Name _____ Period _____ Date _____

7. A ball is kicked off a cliff with an initial horizontal velocity of 11 m/s.

   a. Write parametric equations to model the ball's motion.

   b. If the cliff is 130 m high, where and when will the ball hit the ground?

8. Consider the system of equations

$$\begin{cases} a + b - c = -10 \\ 2a + 2b - 3c = -23 \\ 2a + b + c = -2 \end{cases}$$

   a. Write one or more matrices to represent the system.

   b. Solve the system using a method of your choice. Show your work, and describe your procedure.

9. An object attached to the end of a spring bounces up and down. It reaches a point 12 cm from the floor at its low point and 18 cm from the floor at its high point. It reaches the low point 7 times each second. At time 0, the object is 18 cm above the floor and heading down.

   a. Write an equation that models the position of the object.

   b. Find the object's height at 0.8 s.

   c. Find the first four times the object is at height 14 cm.

10. Solve. Give answers to the nearest 0.001.

   a. $13 + 5(3.8)^x = 21$ **b.** $\log(x + 2) - \log(x - 4) = 1$

   c. $\log_4 37 = x$ **d.** $10^{2x-1} + 10^x = 100$

11. The cost of mailing a 1-ounce letter increased nine times between 1975 and 2002.

Year	1975	1978	1981	1985	1988	1991	1995	1999	2001	2002
Cost ($)	0.13	0.15	0.20	0.22	0.25	0.29	0.32	0.33	0.34	0.37

(*www.infoplease.com*)

   a. Find the median-median line for the (*year, cost*) data. Use 75 to represent the year 1975, and so on.

   b. Find the sum of the residuals for the median-median line. What does this tell you about how well the line fits the data?

   c. Find the slope and *y*-intercept for your model. What is the real-world meaning of the slope and *y*-intercept?

(continued)

Name_____ Period_____ Date_____

12. Write an equation for the quadratic function shown in each form.

    a. Factored form

    b. General form

    c. Vertex form

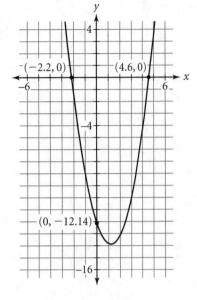

13. The land area and population of the six inhabited continents in the year 2000 are given in the table. Find the correlation coefficient, r, for these data. What does this tell you?

Continent	Africa	Asia	Australia	Europe	North America	South America
Land area (km²)	30,065,000	44,579,000	7,687,000	9,938,000	24,256,000	17,819,000
Population (thousands)	805,243	3,688,072	19,164	728,981	480,545	346,504

(New York Times Almanac 2002)

14. Eureka High has a senior class of 85 students.

    a. In how many ways can a committee of three students be formed?

    b. In how many ways can a student government consisting of a president, vice president, and treasurer be formed?

CHAPTER 0 · Test

1. Possible answer: $(10, -11)$

2. Possible answer:

3. $239

4. Tom: tennis, music, youngest; Harry: football, science, middle; Bob: track, Latin, oldest

5. a. $x^2 - 49$ **b.** $5y - 60 + zy - 12z$
   c. $m^2 - 2mp + p^2$

6. a. 7 **b.** $\frac{4}{5}$ **c.** -1

7. a. $\sqrt{117}$ cm   **b.** $5\sqrt{2}$ in.   **c.** 0.8 cm

8. a. 21 **b.** 3 **c.** 256

9. a. z^6 **b.** $\frac{1}{t^3}$, or t^{-3}
   c. $96y^{15}$ **d.** x

10. a. -3 **b.** $\frac{2}{3}$ **c.** 5 or -3

11. a. $9x - 5$ **b.** $x^2 + 10$ **c.** $\frac{7}{x + 1}$

12. 16.1 ft/s

CHAPTER 0 · Constructive Assessment Options

Scoring rubrics

1. 5 Points

Albert: 9 pounds; Bob: 15 pounds; explanation and work are clear and correct. Possible work and explanation:

Let a be the weight that Albert is carrying; let b be the weight that Bob is carrying. Use the information given to write a system of equations.

$$\begin{cases} a + \frac{1}{3}a = \frac{1}{2}(a + b) \\ b + 3 = \frac{3}{4}(a + b) \end{cases} \quad \text{Original system.}$$

First eliminate fractions by multiplying the first equation by 6 and the second equation by 4; then combine like terms.

$$\begin{cases} 5a - 3b = 0 \\ 3a - b = 12 \end{cases} \quad \text{Reduced system.}$$

$$5a - 3b = 0 \qquad \text{The first equation.}$$
$$\underline{9a - 3b = 36} \qquad \begin{array}{l}\text{Multiply both sides of the} \\ \text{second equation by 3.}\end{array}$$
$$-4a = -36 \qquad \text{Subtract the equations.}$$
$$a = 9 \qquad \text{Solve for } a.$$
$$9 + \frac{1}{3}(9) = \frac{1}{2}(9 + b) \qquad \begin{array}{l}\text{Substitute 9 for } a \text{ in the first} \\ \text{equation.}\end{array}$$
$$b = 15 \qquad \text{Solve for } b.$$

Albert is carrying 9 pounds. Bob is carrying 15 pounds.

3 Points
One of the equations is incorrect, or an error was made in the solution.

1 Point
The problem is attempted, but little correct work is shown.

2. 5 Points
  a. Eight pieces; eight with crust

  b. There are 18 different ways to slice the pizza. The possibilities are shown below. Each is labeled with the number of pieces and the number of pieces with crust.

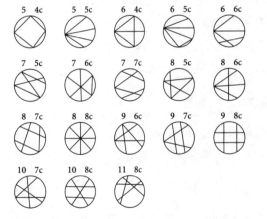

3 Points
The answer to part a is correct. Part b shows about ten different ways.

1 Point
The answer to part a is correct. Part b shows only a few different ways.

CHAPTER 1 • Quiz 1

1. Geometric; $12, 3, \frac{3}{4}, \frac{3}{16}$

2. Arithmetic; $11, 4, -3, -10$

3. $u_1 = 1$ and $u_n = -2 \cdot u_{n-1}$ where $n \geq 2$; $u_{10} = -512$

4. $u_1 = 20$ and $u_n = u_{n-1} - 2.5$ where $n \geq 2$; $u_{12} = -7.5$

5. 120 is the starting height, and 0.25 means that the rebound height decreases by 25% with each bounce.

6. a. ACME: $u_1 = 40{,}000$ and $u_n = (1 + 0.05)u_{n-1}$ where $n \geq 2$

   Widget.com: $u_1 = 40{,}000$ and $u_n = u_{n-1} + 2500$ where $n \geq 2$

   b.

	Salary	
Year	ACME, Inc.	Widget.com
1	$40,000	$40,000
2	$42,000	$42,500
3	$44,100	$45,000
4	$46,305	$47,500
5	$48,620.25	$50,000

   c. In the 11th year

CHAPTER 1 • Quiz 2

1. a. $u_0 = 400$ and $u_n = (1 - 0.20)u_{n-1} + 120$ where $n \geq 1$

   b. 586

   c. The number of bikes will level off at 600.

2. Geometric, decreasing, nonlinear

3. Shifted geometric, increasing, nonlinear

4. Arithmetic, increasing, linear

5. $28,465.94

CHAPTER 1 • Test

1. a. $\{6, 11, 16, 21, 26, 31, 36\}$

   b. $u_1 = 6$ and $u_n = u_{n-1} + 5$ where $n \geq 2$

   c. 106

   d. Figure 42

2. a. Geometric; there is a constant ratio of 3.

   b. $u_1 = 0.01$ and $u_n = 3 \cdot u_{n-1}$ where $n \geq 2$

   c. 65.61

   d. 14th term

3. a. $164,818.57   b. $191,141.58

4. $648.60

5. About 2.592 million; about 3 million

6. Sample answers:

   a. $u_0 = 10$ and $u_n = 0.7u_{n-1}$ where $n \geq 1$

   b. $u_0 = 10$ and $u_n = u_{n-1} + 7$ where $n \geq 1$

   c. $u_0 = 10$ and $u_n = 0.8u_{n-1} + 4$ where $n \geq 1$

CHAPTER 1 • Constructive Assessment Options

SCORING RUBRICS

1. 5 Points

Answers are correct. Explanations are clear, logical, and correct.

a. 4, 16, 52, 160, 484, 1456

b. 12, 36, 108, 324, 972

c. Geometric; $u_0 = 12$ and $u_n = 3u_{n-1}$ where $n \geq 1$. Possible comparison: In the recursive rules for both sequences, the previous term is multiplied by 3. In the recursive rule for the original sequence, 4 is added to the product. In the rule for the sequence of differences, no constant is added to the product. In other words, the rule for the sequence of differences is the "geometric" part of the rule for the shifted geometric sequence.

d. $u_0 = 1640$ and $u_n = 0.25u_{n-1} - 2$ where $n \geq 1$. Possible explanation: The starting term is 1640. The sequence of differences, $-1232, -308, -77, -19.25, -4.8125$, is a geometric sequence with common ratio 0.25. So the geometric part of the original sequence also has common ratio 0.25. Multiply the starting term by 0.25: $1640 \cdot 0.25 = 410$. To get 408, you must subtract 2. So the rule is $u_n = 0.25u_{n-1} - 2$. This rule works to generate the other terms.

3 Points

The answers to parts a and b are complete and correct. The sequence is correct in part c, but the explanation is not completely clear. The answer to part d is attempted but incorrect.

1 Point

The answers to parts a and b are correct. The answers to parts c and d are missing or incorrect.

2. 5 Points

Answers are correct and complete. Explanations are clear, correct, and logical.

a. Plan A: $u_1 = 50$ and $u_n = u_{n-1} + 5$ where $n \geq 2$; plan B: $u_1 = 50$ and $u_n = u_{n-1}(1 + 0.05)$ where $n \geq 2$

Discovering Advanced Algebra Assessment Resources B
©2004 Key Curriculum Press

b.

	Pay ($)		
Week	Plan A	Plan B	Plan A − Plan B
5	70	60.78	9.22
10	95	77.57	17.43
15	120	99.00	21.00
20	145	126.35	18.65
25	170	161.25	8.74

c. Plan A gives a greater weekly salary at first. In week 28, the salary from plan B becomes greater.

d. Sample answer: I would think about how long I intended to keep the job. If I planned to work for fewer than 28 weeks, I would definitely take plan A. If I planned to make a long-term commitment to the job, I would take plan B. After 28 weeks, plan B pays more, but someone working under plan A would have already collected much more money, so it would take several weeks after week 28 for the cumulative total for plan B to catch up with the cumulative total for plan A.

3 Points
The answers to parts a–c are complete and correct. The answer to part d is missing, unclear, or illogical.

1 Point
The answers to parts a and b are complete and correct. The answer to part c is incorrect. The answer to part d is missing, unclear, or illogical.

3. 5 Points
Answers are correct. Explanations are clear, correct, and logical.

a. $81,196; $38,589.26; $36,871.41

b. $\frac{93,995 - 81,196}{93,995} = 13.6\%$; $\frac{38,589.26 - 36,871.41}{38,589.26} = 4.5\%$

c. 16 years

d. $30,000; explanations will vary. Students may have used a calculator or they may have solved the equation $y = (1 - 0.2)x + 6000$.

e.

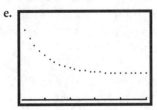

[0, 25, 5, 0, 100000, 100000]

3 Points
The answers to parts a, c, and e are complete and correct. In part b, the correct calculations are attempted, but the answers may be incorrect due to computation error. Part d is attempted, but the procedure is not clear.

1 Point
The answers to parts a and e are correct. The answers to the other parts are missing or include significant errors.

CHAPTER 2 · Quiz 1

1. Sample answer: {5, 10, 15, 17, 17, 18, 18, 20}

2. a. Mr. Rivera: 9, 10, 11.5, 14, 17; Ms. Jensen: 0, 5, 9, 15, 20

b.

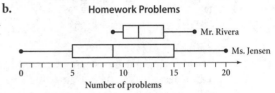

Homework Problems

c. Sample answer: Ms. Jensen varied the number of problems she assigned much more than Mr. Rivera did. Mr. Rivera assigned nine problems or more every day, while Ms. Jensen assigned that many on only half the days. On about one-quarter of the days, Ms. Jensen assigned five problems or fewer, while Mr. Rivera never assigned fewer than nine problems.

3. Mr. Rivera: 2.5; Ms. Jensen: 6.9; the data for Ms. Jensen are more spread out around the mean than are the data for Mr. Rivera.

CHAPTER 2 · Quiz 2

1. 21 theaters

2. 50 cents

3. About 14%

4. 19th percentile

5. Estimates will vary, but should be between $2.00 and $2.49. Sample explanation: Because there are 21 values, the median is the 11th value, which is in the bin that includes values from $2.00 to $2.49.

CHAPTER 2 · Test

1. Sample answer: The values in set A are generally lower than those in set B, with the minimum, first quartile, median, third quartile, and maximum in set A all lower than the corresponding values in set B. The data in set A are not as spread out as the data in set B. The data in set A are fairly symmetric, while the data in set B are skewed, with the values above the median more spread out than the values below the median.

2. Sample answer:

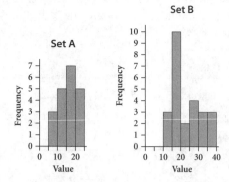

Set A

Set B

3. $\bar{x} \approx 91.9$, *median* = 80.5, *mode* = 73, *s* = 42.8; choices of measures that best characterize the data will vary, but because one very large value (250) pulls up the mean and because the mode is the smallest value in the data set, the median is the measure of center that best characterizes the data.

4. Sample answer: The data set {17, 18, 18, 19, 19, 25, 36, 40, 42} has a median of 19 and a mean of 26.

5. Histogram A sample answer: If you generated thousands of random numbers in a given range, the results should be fairly evenly distributed. If you made a histogram of the data, each bin would include about the same number of values, so the bars would all be about the same height.

Histogram B sample answer: If a teacher gave a very difficult test, a few students who studied very hard would get high scores, but most students would do poorly, with a lot of students getting very low scores. If you graphed the scores in a histogram, the bars for the lower scores would be tall, and the heights would decrease for higher scores.

6. a. $\bar{x} \approx 181.3$, $s \approx 66.3$

  b. 101, 122, 175.5, 214, 318

  c. 19 movies

  d. 85th percentile

  e. Graph choice will vary, but should be justified with logical reasoning.

  Box plot:

Domestic Gross of Top Movies

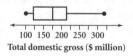

Total domestic gross ($ million)

Histogram:

Domestic Gross of Top Movies

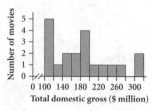

Total domestic gross ($ million)

  f. Articles will vary, but should include relevant statistics.

CHAPTER 2 · Constructive Assessment Options

SCORING RUBRICS

1. 5 Points

Answers are complete and correct.

  a. Females: *mean* ≈ 6.65, *median* = 7, *mode* = 7; males: *mean* ≈ 9.56, *median* = 10, *mode* = 10

  b. Answers may vary, but should be justified with statistics. Sample answer: For the females, I think the typical shoe size is 7 because it is both the median and the mode, and it is fairly close to the mean. For males, I think the typical shoe size is 10 for the same reasons.

  c. Females: 4.5, 5.75, 7, 7.5, 9; males: 7, 8.5, 10, 10.5, 12

Eleventh-Grade Shoe Sizes

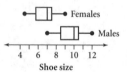

Shoe size

Comparisons will vary, but should be based on information from the box plot and the measures of center. Sample answer: Both plots are skewed left, so shoe sizes below the median are more spread out than shoe sizes above the median. The median shoe size for females is three sizes smaller than the median shoe size for males. The smallest shoe size for males is the same as the median shoe size for females. The upper 75% of female sizes overlap with the lower 50% of male sizes.

3 Points

The answers to parts a and b are correct. The five-number summaries and box plots in part c are correct, but only one meaningful comparison is made.

1 Point

The answer to part a is correct. The sizes chosen in part b are reasonable, but the explanations are missing or unclear. The answer to part c is missing.

2. 5 Points

Answers are correct and complete. Explanations are clear, logical, and based on statistics.

a. **San Francisco Gasoline Prices**

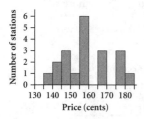

b. *mean* = 160, *median* = 159.9, *mode* = 159.9

c. 44 cents

d. The histogram would probably have a similar shape, but would be shifted to the left by 25 cents.

e. Sample answer: From the histogram, you can see the price spread. There seems to be as many stations with cheaper gas as with more expensive gas. It is worth looking for a bargain as long as you don't drive around with an almost empty tank, which might force you to stop at a more expensive station.

3 Points

The answers to parts a–c are complete and correct. The answer to either part d or part e is correct, but the other answer is missing, incorrect, or illogical.

1 Point

Two of the answers in parts a–c are correct. Parts d and e are not attempted.

3. 5 Points

Answers are correct. Explanations are clear, correct, and logical.

a. **Heights of Basketball Players**

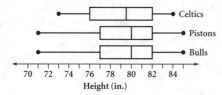

b. Celtics: 73, 76, 79.5, 82, 84; Pistons: 71, 77, 80, 82, 85; Bulls: 71, 77, 80, 82, 85

c. Celtics: 79; Pistons: 79.13; Bulls: 79.08; the means are virtually the same.

d. Celtics: 3.30; Pistons: 4.21; Bulls: 4.08

e. Sample answer: The five-number summaries (and thus the box plots) for the Pistons and Bulls are

identical. The heights for the Celtics have a smaller range than for the other two teams. The standard deviations indicate that the heights for the Pistons are the most spread out, while the heights for the Celtics are the most uniform. All the plots are skewed left, indicating that, for all three teams, there is more variation among the heights less than the median. The shortest 25% and tallest 25% of the heights are less spread out for the Celtics than for the other two teams. However, the middle 50% of the heights are more spread out for the Celtics than for the other two teams.

3 Points

The answers to parts a–d are correct. Part e includes only one or two correct statements.

1 Point

At least two of the answers in parts a–d are correct. The statements in part e are missing or incorrect.

4. 5 Points

Answers are complete and correct.

a. 22,500 students

b. 242,500 students

c. 94th percentile

d. 76th percentile

e. 99th percentile; this means that Cheon did better than 99% of the students taking the exam, and the other 1% of the students did as well as Cheon did.

f. The first histogram should show that half the students (50,000) scored perfect tests. The second histogram should show that 99,000 students got one or none of the questions correct. Sample answers:

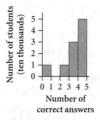
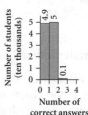

3 Points

The answers to parts a–e are correct, although the explanation in part e may be incomplete or unclear. Part f is attempted, but the answer includes significant errors.

1 Point

The answers to parts a and b are correct. At least two of the other parts are attempted, but the answers are incorrect.

CHAPTER 3 • Quiz 1

1. $u_n = 11 - 6n$

2. $y = -7 + 4.25x$

3. a. Possible answer: $\hat{y} - 135 = 6.88(x - 1999)$

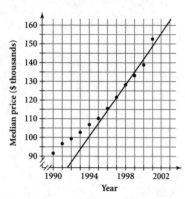

Median Home Prices

b. Possible answer: about $279,500

CHAPTER 3 • Quiz 2

1. $\hat{y} = \frac{37}{3} - \frac{7}{6}x$, or $\hat{y} = 12.33 - 1.17x$

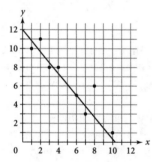

2. Answers may vary slightly, depending on the form of the equation students use and how they round. Residuals: $-1.17, -0.83, 0.33, -1.17, 0.33, 3.00, 1.00, -0.33$; sum of residuals: 1.17

3. $s \approx 1.51$; the values predicted by the equation are generally within 1.51 of the actual value.

4. Sample answer: The root mean square error, 1.51, is fairly large relative to the data values, indicating that the fit is not particularly good. Three of the individual residuals are greater than 1, which is large for this data set. The sum of the residuals is positive, indicating that the model tends to underestimate the values.

CHAPTER 3 • Quiz 3

1. It depends on how many people will be at the party. For 18 people or fewer, Posh Parties is less expensive. For more than 18 people, Marvelous Meals costs less.

2. $(-3, -3)$ **3.** $(7, -2)$

4. C

CHAPTER 3 • Test

1. a. $u_n = -2.25 + 1.25n$ **b.** $u_{47} = 56.5$

   c. $n = 53$

2. a. $u_0 = 2$ and $u_n = u_{n-1} - 3$ where $n \geq 1$

   b. $y = 2 - 3x$

3. a. Possible answer:

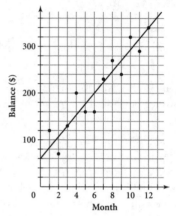

Julia's Account

b. Possible answer: $\hat{y} - 130 = \frac{70}{3}(x - 3)$, or $\hat{y} = \frac{70}{3}x + 60$

   c. Slopes will vary. The slope is the approximate amount by which Julia's balance increases each month.

   d. y-intercepts will vary. The y-intercept represents Julia's balance at the beginning of the year.

4. a. $\hat{y} = -675.7227 + 0.3445x$

   b. $20.17; extrapolation, because it involves predicting a value beyond the given data values

   c. $8.11; interpolation, because it involves predicting a value between the given data values

   d. Residuals: $0.2877, 0.0687, -0.0803, -0.1493, -0.0083, 0.2727, 0.6037, 0.5547, 0.3057, 0.1367, 0.1777, 0.0487, -0.0903, -0.0793, 0.1917, 0.4727$; sum of residuals: 2.7132

   e. $s \approx 0.30$; this means that the earnings predicted by the model are generally within $0.30 of the actual value.

   f. Sample answer: The model is a fairly good fit. The root mean square error is relatively small compared to the data values. However, the sum of the residuals is a relatively large positive number, indicating that the model tends to underestimate the earnings.

5. a. $(-6, 10)$ **b.** $(-2, 7)$

Discovering Advanced Algebra Assessment Resources B
©2004 Key Curriculum Press

CHAPTER 3 · Constructive Assessment Options

Scoring rubrics

1. 5 Points
Answers and explanations are clear, complete, and correct.

a.

U. S. Life Expectancy

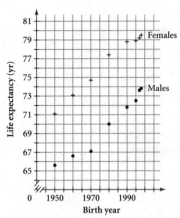

Birth year

b. Answers will vary. Possible answer: Males: Using (1960, 66.6) and (1980, 70) gives the equation $\hat{y} = \frac{3.4}{20}(x - 1980) + 70$, or $\hat{y} = 0.17x - 266.6$. Females: Using (1960, 73.1) and (1995, 78.9) gives the equation $\hat{y} = \frac{5.8}{35}(x - 1960) + 73.1$, or $\hat{y} = 0.1657x - 251.7$.

c. Sample answer: The slopes are almost the same, with the slope for the male line slightly greater. The slope represents the amount that life expectancy increases each time the birth year increases by 1.

d. Predictions are correct based on the model. Using the equations in part b, the life expectancy for a male born in 2050 will be 81.9 years, and the life expectancy for a female will be 88.0 years.

e. Intersection point is correct based on equations found in part b. The linear model is unrealistic to make predictions for 2500. Possible explanation: The two lines intersect at about (3465, 322), which would mean that both a male and a female born in 3465 would have a life expectancy of 322 years. Obviously, a linear model will break down long before 3465. According to this model, in 2500, a male might expect to live for 158.4 years and a female for 162.6 years. This seems unlikely. A linear model is unrealistic for making predictions in the far future because it predicts that life expectancy increases indefinitely at a constant rate. Realistically, the increase in life expectancy will probably slow down and level off at some point.

3 Points
The answers to parts a, b, and d are correct. The interpretation of the slope in part c is missing or incorrect. The intersection point in part e is correct,

but the interpretations and explanations are incomplete or incorrect.

1 Point
The answer to part a is correct. One of the equations in part b is incorrect. The answers to part d are correct based on the equations in part b. Answers to the other parts include significant errors and omissions.

2. 5 Points
Answers are correct and complete. Explanations are clear, complete, and logical.

a. Bill's equation: $\hat{y} = \frac{3.4}{6}(x - 1) + 2.4$, or $\hat{y} = 0.57x + 1.83$

Sara's equation: $\hat{y} = \frac{1.6}{3}(x - 2) + 3$, or $\hat{y} = 0.53x + 1.93$

b.

x	y	Bill's $\hat{y}$	Bill's residuals	Sara's $\hat{y}$	Sara's residuals
1	2.4	2.4	0	2.46	−0.06
2	3.0	2.97	0.03	2.99	0.01
3	4.0	3.54	0.46	3.52	0.48
4	4.2	4.11	0.09	4.05	0.15
5	4.6	4.68	−0.08	4.58	0.02
6	5.5	5.25	0.25	5.11	0.39
7	5.8	5.82	−0.02	5.64	0.16

c. Bill: 0.24 cm; Sara: 0.29 cm

d. Bill's line is a better fit. It has a smaller root mean square error and a more even distribution of points above and below the line.

e. Answers and explanations will vary, but the new model should have a smaller root mean square error than the original model. Sample answer: Bill's residuals are mostly positive, so by shifting Bill's line up slightly, we can improve the fit. To move the line up, increase the y-intercept. The equation $\hat{y} = 0.57x + 1.93$ has a root mean square error of 0.21 cm.

3 Points
The answers to parts a–c are correct. The answers to parts d and e may be missing or incorrect.

1 Point
The equations in part a are correct. Several of the residuals in part b are incorrect. The answers to parts c–e are missing or incorrect.

3. 5 Points
Answers are correct and complete.

a. $\hat{y} = -1013.781 + 0.517x$

b. $0.59

c. $25.39

d. The hourly costs in 2010 will be between 25.39 − 0.59 = \$24.80 and 25.39 + 0.59 = \$25.98.

3 Points

The answers to parts a and c are correct. The procedure used in part b is correct, but a minor error leads to an incorrect answer. Part d is attempted but not correct.

1 Point

The answer to part a is correct. The answers to the other parts are missing or incorrect.

4. 5 Points

Answers are correct and complete. Explanations are clear, correct, and logical.

a. For both sequences, $u_{91} = 108$. Possible explanation: The explicit formula for the first sequence is $u_n = 1.4n - 19.4$. The explicit formula for the second sequence is $u_n = 1.1n + 7.9$. We want to find the value of n for which $1.4n - 19.4 = 1.1n + 7.9$. Solving for n gives $n = 91$. Substituting into either original equation gives $u_n = 108$. So for both sequences, $u_{91} = 108$.

b. Possible answer: The explicit formula for the first sequence is $u_n = 2.3n + 3.7$. The explicit formula for the second sequence is $u_n = 3n - 33$. Solving $2.3n + 3.7 = 3n - 33$ gives $n = 52\frac{3}{7}$. However, n is a term number, so it must be a whole number. So there is no term number for which the two sequences have the same value.

3 Points

The answer and explanation for part a are correct. Either the intersection point *or* the explanation in part b is incorrect.

1 Point

Solutions to parts a and b are attempted and involve writing explicit formulas. However, at least one of the intersection points is incorrect, and the explanations are missing or include significant errors.

CHAPTERS 1–3 · Exam

1. a. Arithmetic; linear; 13, 4, −5, −14, −23

b. Geometric; curved; 125, 100, 80, 64, 51.2

2. a. $u_0 = 17,500$ and $u_n = (1 - 0.18)u_{n-1}$ where $n \geq 1$

b. $6488

c. 7 years

3. Possible answer:

a. $u_1 = 40$ and $u_n = 1.15u_{n-1}$ where $n \geq 2$

b. About 753

c. After 56 days

4. a. About 365 mg

b. 375 mg

5. a. 6,459; 26,277; 36,484; 57,418; 146,571

b. Range: 140,112; *IQR*: 31,141

c.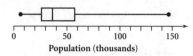
Population of Vermont Counties

d. Skewed right

e. Yes; Chittenden

6. a. $\bar{x} \approx 43,488$; $s \approx 34,385$

b. Essex, Grand Isle, and Chittenden

c. 43rd percentile

d. Sample answer:

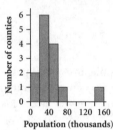
Population of Vermont Counties

7. a. (20, 12)   **b.** (−5, 9)

8. a. $u_0 = -19$ and $u_n = u_{n-1} + 7$ where $n \geq 1$

b. $u_n = -19 + 7n$

c. 170

d. The slope would be 7 and the *y*-intercept would be −19.

9. a. The data appear somewhat linear.

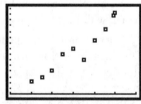

[1950, 2010, 10, 0, 30, 2]

b. $\hat{y} = -1244.838 + 0.636x$

c. The slope, 0.636, means that the amount of energy imported increases by about 0.636 quadrillion Btu each year.

d. 58.962 quadrillion Btu (or 59.234 quadrillion BTU if the median-median line is used unrounded)

e. The residuals are 2.508, 1.018, 0.308, 2.848, 1.528, −5.522, −1.852, −1.412, 1.024, 1.358. The root mean square error is about 2.66. This means that the energy consumption values predicted by the model are generally within 2.66 quadrillion Btu of the actual value.

CHAPTER 4 • Quiz 1

1.

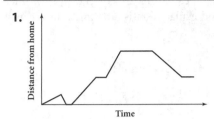

2. a. B   **b.** A   **c.** C

3. a. Yes   **b.** No   **c.** Yes

4. a. -2 **b.** $\dfrac{3}{11}$ **c.** -6 **d.** -3

CHAPTER 4 • Quiz 2

1. $y = -3 + 6(x - 9)$, or $y = -57 + 6x$

2. a. $y = f(x + 4)$ **b.** $y = f(x) - 1$

   c. $y = -5 + f(x - 2)$

3. a. It is the graph of $y = x^2$ shifted right 2 units.

   b. It is the graph of $y = x^2$ shifted left 5 units and down 1 unit.

   c. It is the graph of $y = x^2$ shifted up 4 units and then reflected across the x-axis.

   d. It is the graph of $y = x^2$ reflected across the x-axis and then shifted up 4 units.

4. a. $y = \sqrt{x - 3}$

   b. $y = \sqrt{-x}$

   c. $y = -\sqrt{x} + 2$

CHAPTER 4 • Quiz 3

1. a. $y = 0.5(x + 2)^2$ **b.** $y = |2x|$ or $y = 2|x|$

   c. $y = -|x - 2| + 3$

2. $\left(\dfrac{x-4}{3}\right)^2 + \left(\dfrac{y+5}{4}\right)^2 = 1$; $y = -5 + 4\sqrt{1 - \left(\dfrac{x-4}{3}\right)^2}$

   and $y = -5 - 4\sqrt{1 - \left(\dfrac{x-4}{3}\right)^2}$

3. a. $f(g(-2)) = -4$; $g(f(-2)) = 0$

   b. $f(g(x)) = |x + 1|^2 - 5 = (x + 1)^2 - 5 = x^2 + 2x - 4$; $g(f(x)) = |x^2 - 4|$

   c.

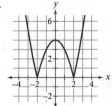

CHAPTER 4 • Test

1. a.

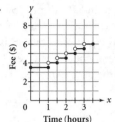

   b. The relation is a function because for each parking time there is exactly one charge.

2. a. $f(g(-2)) = -\dfrac{7}{5}$

   b. $h(g(5)) = 5041$

   c. $g(f(x)) = 3\left(-\dfrac{x}{5} + 1\right)^2 = \dfrac{3x^2}{25} - \dfrac{6x}{5} + 3$

3.   **4.**

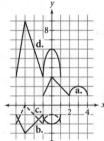   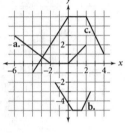

5. Possible answer: $y = 0.75(x - 3)^2 - 5$

6. a. Parent: $y = |x|$; equation: $y = \dfrac{1}{2}|x - 1| - 2$

   b. Parent: $y = \sqrt{1 - x^2}$; equation:
$$y = -4\sqrt{1 - \dfrac{(x + 2)^2}{4}} + 1$$

   c. Parent: $y = |x|$; equation: $y = -|x - 3| + 3$

   d. Parent: $y = \sqrt{x}$; equation: $y = -\sqrt{1 - x} + 1$

7. $y = \pm 7\sqrt{1 - \left(\dfrac{x - 1}{3}\right)^2}$

8. $x = 7$ or $x = -17$

CHAPTER 4 • Constructive Assessment Options

SCORING RUBRICS

1. 5 Points
Table is complete and correct. *(See table at bottom of next page.)*

3 Points
There are between 5 and 10 errors among the 31 answers in the table.

1 Point
There are between 15 and 20 errors among the 31 answers in the table.

2. 5 Points

a. *(See table at bottom of page.)*

b. The order matters for A and B but not for C and D. The final equations when A is applied first are different from the final equations when B is applied first, but the final equations when C is applied first are the same as the final equations when D is applied first.

3 Points

Six of the eight final equations are correct. One of the conclusions and explanations is complete and correct. The other conclusion and explanation are attempted, but are incomplete or incorrect.

1 Point

Four of the final equations are correct. At least one conclusion and explanation is attempted, but it may not be correct.

3. 5 Points

Answers are correct and complete.

a. $\left(\dfrac{x}{4}\right)^2 + \left(\dfrac{y}{4}\right)^2 = 1$ b. $x^2 + y^2 = 16$

c.

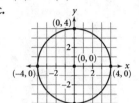

Chapter 4, Constructive Assessment Options, Problems 1, 2a

1.

Parent equation	Transformations in words	Images of $(0, 0)$ and $(1, 1)$	Image equation showing transformations	Image equation solved for y
$y = x$	**Translate right 1 unit and up 6 units.**	$(0, 0) \rightarrow (1, 6)$ $(1, 1) \rightarrow (2, 7)$	$y - 6 = x - 1$	$y = x + 5$
$y = x$	Stretch horizontally by a factor of $\frac{1}{3}$ and vertically by a factor of 2.	$(0, 0) \rightarrow (0, 0)$ $(1, 1) \rightarrow \left(\frac{1}{3}, 2\right)$	$\frac{1}{2}y = 3x$	$y = 6x$
$y = x$	**Reflect across the x-axis, and stretch vertically by a factor of $\frac{2}{3}$.**	$(0, 0) \rightarrow (0, 0)$ $(1, 1) \rightarrow \left(1, -\frac{2}{3}\right)$	$\frac{3}{2}y = -x$, or $-\frac{3}{2}y = x$	$y = -\frac{2}{3}x$
$y = x^2$	Reflect across the x-axis.	$(0, 0) \rightarrow (0, 0)$ $(1, 1) \rightarrow (1, -1)$	$y = -x^2$, or $-y = x^2$	$y = -x^2$
$y = \|x\|$	**Translate right 4 units and down 6 units.**	$(0, 0) \rightarrow (4, -6)$ $(1, 1) \rightarrow (5, -5)$	$y + 6 = \|x - 4\|$	$y = \|x - 4\| - 6$
$y = \|x\|$	Translate left 3 units, and stretch vertically by a factor of $\frac{1}{3}$.	$(0, 0) \rightarrow (-3, 0)$ $(1, 1) \rightarrow \left(-2, \frac{1}{3}\right)$	$3y = \|x + 3\|$	$y = \frac{1}{3}\|x + 3\|$
$y = \sqrt{x}$	**Reflect across the y-axis, and stretch horizontally by a factor of 2.**	$(0, 0) \rightarrow (0, 0)$ $(1, 1) \rightarrow (-2, 1)$	$y = \sqrt{-\frac{1}{2}x}$	$y = \sqrt{-\frac{1}{2}x}$
$y = \sqrt{x}$	Translate left 5 units and down 7 units.	$(0, 0) \rightarrow (-5, -7)$ $(1, 1) \rightarrow (-4, -6)$	$y + 7 = \sqrt{x + 5}$	$y = \sqrt{x + 5} - 7$

2. a.

	$y = \|x\|$	$y = \sqrt{x}$
Apply A to the parent function.	$y = \|x - 4\| - 1$	$y = \sqrt{x - 4} - 1$
Apply B to the image under A.	$y = -\|x - 4\| + 1$	$y = -\sqrt{x - 4} + 1$
Apply B to the parent function.	$y = -\|x\|$	$y = -\sqrt{x}$
Apply A to the image under B.	$y = -\|x - 4\| - 1$	$y = -\sqrt{x - 4} - 1$
Apply C to the parent function.	$y = \frac{1}{2}\|x\|$	$y = \frac{1}{2}\sqrt{x}$
Apply D to the image under C.	$y = \frac{1}{2}\|x - 5\|$	$y = \frac{1}{2}\sqrt{x - 5}$
Apply D to the parent function.	$y = \|x - 5\|$	$y = \sqrt{x - 5}$
Apply C to the image under D.	$y = \frac{1}{2}\|x - 5\|$	$y = \frac{1}{2}\sqrt{x - 5}$

Discovering Advanced Algebra Assessment Resources B
©2004 Key Curriculum Press

d. $\left(\dfrac{x+2}{4}\right)^2 + \left(\dfrac{y-3}{4}\right)^2 = 1$

e.

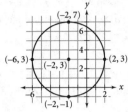

f. $\left(-2-\sqrt{7},\,0\right), \left(-2+\sqrt{7},\,0\right), \left(0,\,3-2\sqrt{3}\right),$ and $\left(0,\,3+2\sqrt{3}\right)$

g. $\left(\dfrac{x-2}{3}\right)^2 + \left(\dfrac{y-5}{3}\right)^2 = 1$, or $(x-2)^2 + (y-5)^2 = 9$

3 Points

The answer to part f is incorrect or missing. There are one or two other minor errors.

1 Point

The answers to parts c and f are incorrect or missing. There are four other minor errors.

4. 5 Points

Answers are correct and complete.

a. **i.** Domain: 1 mm $\leq x \leq$ 100 mm; range: $\dfrac{\pi}{6}$ mm$^2 \leq y \leq \dfrac{10000\pi}{6}$ mm^2

ii. $A(x) = \dfrac{1}{6}\pi x^2$

iii.

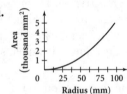

iv. $y = A(x)$ is a vertical stretch of the parent function $y = x^2$ by a factor of $\dfrac{\pi}{6}$.

b. **i.** Domain: $\dfrac{\pi}{6}$ mm$^2 \leq x \leq \dfrac{10000\pi}{6}$ mm^2; range: $\$224.42 \leq y \leq \$94{,}462.78$

ii. $P(x) = 18x + 215$

iii.

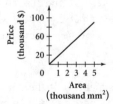

iv. The parent function $y = x$ has been stretched horizontally by a factor of $\dfrac{1}{18}$ and translated up 215 units. (Or, the parent function $y = x$ has been stretched vertically by a factor of 18 and then translated up 215 units.)

c. **i.** $C(x) = P(A(x))$

ii. $C(x) = 3\pi x^2 + 215$

iii. $\$432.15$; $\$32{,}248.78$

iv.

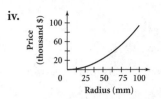

v. The parent function $y = x^2$ has been stretched vertically by a factor of 3π and then translated up 215 units.

3 Points

In parts a and b, the answers to parts i–iii are correct. The answer to part iv is incorrect or missing in either part a or part b. In part c, the answers to three of the five parts are complete and correct.

1 Point

In parts a and b, the answers to parts i–iii are correct, but the answers to part iv are incorrect. The answers to part c include three or more significant errors.

CHAPTER 5 • Quiz 1

1. a. $\$221{,}264$ **b.** 6 years and 8 months

2. a. $-12x^2$ **b.** $3x^{15}$ **c.** $8x^{24}$ **d.** $5x^2$

3. a. $x = -\dfrac{3}{2}$ **b.** $x \approx 2.77$ **c.** $x \approx 17.24$

4. a. y-intercept: 4; ratio: 0.6

b. Possible answer: (2, 1.44); $y = 1.44 \cdot 0.6^{x-2}$

c. Answer depends on equation in part b. Answer based on equation above:

$y = 1.44 \cdot 0.6^{x-2}$	Original equation.
$= 1.44 \cdot 0.6^x \cdot 0.6^{-2}$	Multiplication property of exponents.
$= \dfrac{1.44}{0.6^2} \cdot 0.6^x$	Definition of negative exponent.
$= \dfrac{1.44}{0.36} \cdot 0.6^x$	Evaluate 0.6^2.
$= 4 \cdot 0.6^x$	Divide.

CHAPTER 5 • Quiz 2

1. About 11.4% per year

2. a. Possible equation: $y = 4683.79\left(\dfrac{6267.97}{4683.79}\right)^{(x-5)/5}$, or $y = 4683.79(1.06)^{x-5}$

b. About $\$3500$

c. 6%

3. a. $y = \dfrac{8}{3}(x-4)$, or $y = \dfrac{8}{3}x - \dfrac{32}{3}$; yes

b. $y = -2 \pm \sqrt{x}$; no

c. $(-2, -4), (-1, -2), (0, 0), (1, 2), (2, 4)$; yes

CHAPTER 5 · Quiz 3

1. a. $x \approx -1.08$ **b.** $x \approx 3.90$ **c.** $x \approx -12.94$

2. 7.47 years, or about 7 years and 6 months

3. a. True   **b.** False; $\log x^7 = 7 \log x$

   c. True   **d.** False; $\log 56 = \log 7 + \log 8$

4. 10^{-3} W/cm^2

CHAPTER 5 · Test

1. Possible answers:

   a. $\sqrt[5]{m^4}$ **b.** $\log b^4$ **c.** $\dfrac{\log 9}{\log x}$

   d. $\dfrac{z^3}{y^2}$ **e.** 3^{x+2y} **f.** $\log 21$

2. a. $x \approx 9.38$ **b.** $x = 1$ **c.** $x \approx 0.38$

   d. $x \approx -15.25$ **e.** $x \approx \pm 2.09$ **f.** $x = 15$

3. $y = 280\left(\dfrac{17.5}{280}\right)^{(x-1)/4}$, or equivalent equation

4. About 6.1%

5. In 6.58 years, or about 6 years and 7 months

6. a. $f^{-1}(x) = \left(\dfrac{x-3}{5}\right)^2 + 2$ for $x \geq 3$

   b. $f^{-1}(4) = \dfrac{51}{25}$

   c. $f(f^{-1}(5)) = 5$

7. a. $a = 6.75$; $b = 23.45$

   b. ≈ 0.52; This is the amount of time, in hours, a customer can use electricity for free. (For amounts less than 0.52 hour, the company would actually owe the customer money!)

   c. $49.26

   d. About 2.25 hours, or about 2 hours 15 minutes

8. a.

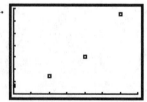

[0, 35, 5, 0, 1750, 250]

   b.

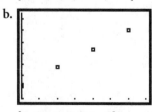

[0, 35, 5, 2, 3.5, .2]

Possible explanation: If the tuition and fees are growing exponentially, then the data can be modeled by an equation of the form $y = ab^x$. Taking the logarithm of both sides gives $\log y = \log a + x \log b$. This is a linear equation.

So if the relationship between x and y is exponential, then the relationship between x and $\log y$ will be linear. The plot $(x, \log y)$ clearly shows a linear pattern, providing evidence that the original data are exponential.

   c. $\log \hat{y} = 2.245 + 0.032x$

   d. $\hat{y} = 175.79(1.076)^x$, or $\hat{y} = 175.76(1.077)^x$ if values for the median-median line are used without rounding

   e. About $3292, or $3359 with unrounded values

   f. 2021

   g. Sample answer: The model predicts that the tuition and fees in 1992 came to $881 (or $890 without rounding). This is only $56 (or $47) less than the actual tuition and fees, so the data fit the model fairly well.

CHAPTER 5 · Constructive Assessment Options

SCORING RUBRICS

1. 5 Points

Answers are correct and complete. Explanations are clear, complete, and logical.

   a. Possible answer: $y = 18(0.78)^{x-8}$

   b. Possible answer: $y = 13(0.80)^{x-10} + 1$

   c. The model in part b better represents the situation because of the assumption that the long-run value is one student per computer. The model in part a has a long-run value of 0 students per computer.

   d. Answer depends on the equation found in part b. Using the equation $y = 13(0.80)^{x-10} + 1$, the ratio of students to computers is $f(22) = 1.89$.

   e. Answer depends on the equation found in part b. Using the equation $y = 13(0.80)^{x-10} + 1$, the ratio of students to computers will first be less than 2 in the school year 2004–05; Possible explanation: $f(21) = 2.1167$ and $f(22) = 1.89$, so the number of students per computer will drop to less than 2 in the 22nd year after 1983–84, which is 2004–05.

3 Points

The equations in parts a and b fit the data reasonably well. The answer to part c may or may not be correct. The answers to parts d and e were found using the model in part c (whether or not it was the correct model), but one of the answers is incorrect.

1 Point

The equation in part a is a good fit. The equation in part b is *not* a good fit. The answer to part c is wrong. Parts d and e are attempted, but the answers are not close to the correct answers or are guesses with no work shown.

2. 5 Points

Answers are complete and correct. Explanations are clear, complete, and logical.

a. $y = b(ab^x)$ Vertical stretch of $y = ab^x$ by a factor of b.

$\quad = ab^1b^x$ Commutative property, and $b = b^1$.

$\quad = ab^{x+1}$ Multiplication property of exponents.

The function $y = ab^{(x+1)}$ is a translation of $y = ab^x$ left 1 unit.

b. A translation left 2 units;

$y = 4a(2)^x$ Vertical stretch of $y = a(2)^x$ by a factor of 4.

$\quad = a(2^2)(2^x)$ Rewrite 4 as 2^2; commutative property.

$\quad = a(2)^{x+2}$ Multiplication property of exponents.

$y = a(2)^{x+2}$ is a translation of $y = a(2)^x$ left 2 units.

c. A horizontal translation by $-\dfrac{\log p}{\log 2}$ units (or $-\log_2 p$ units); possible justification: $y = pa(2^x)$ is a vertical stretch of $y = a(2)^x$ by p units. Rewrite p as a power of 2: $p = 2^z$, where $z = \log_2 p = \dfrac{\log p}{\log 2}$. Then

$y = pa(2)^x$ Vertical stretch of $y = a(2)^x$ by a factor of p.

$\quad = a \cdot 2^z \cdot 2^x$ Rewrite p as 2^z; commutative property.

$\quad = a(2)^{x+z}$ Multiplication property of exponents.

$\quad = a(2)^{(x+(\log p/\log 2))}$ Substitute $\dfrac{\log p}{\log 2}$ for z.

$y = a(2)^{(x+(\log p/\log 2))}$ represents a horizontal translation of $y = a(2)^x$ by $-\dfrac{\log p}{\log 2}$ units.

d. A horizontal translation by $-\dfrac{\log p}{\log b}$ units (or $-\log_b p$ units); possible justification: $y = pab^x$ is a vertical stretch of $y = ab^x$ by p units. Rewrite p as a power of b: $p = b^z$, where $z = \log_b p = \dfrac{\log p}{\log b}$. Then

$y = pab^x$ Vertical stretch of $y = ab^x$ by a factor of p.

$\quad = a(b^z)(b^x)$ Rewrite p as b^z; commutative property.

$\quad = ab^{x+z}$ Multiplication property of exponents.

$\quad = ab^{(x+(\log p/\log b))}$ Substitute $\dfrac{\log p}{\log b}$ for z.

$y = ab^{(x+(\log p/\log b))}$ represents a horizontal translation of $y = ab^x$ by $-\dfrac{\log p}{\log b}$ units.

3 Points

The answers to parts a–c are correct.

1 Point

The answers to parts a and b are correct.

3. 5 Points

Answers are correct and complete. Explanations are clear, complete, and logical.

a.

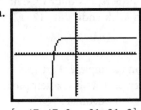

$[-47, 47, 2, -31, 31, 2]$

b. Domain: all real numbers; range: $y < 12$

c. y-intercept: $11\frac{1023}{1024}$; x-intercept: $-1.25\left(\dfrac{\log 12}{\log 2} + 10\right)$. The y-intercept is $f(0)$:

$$f(0) = -2^{-0.8(0)-10} + 12$$
$$= -2^{-10} + 12$$
$$= -\frac{1}{1024} + 12$$
$$= 11\frac{1023}{1024}$$

The x-intercept is the value of x when $f(x) = 0$:

$$0 = -2^{-0.8x-10} + 12$$
$$2^{-0.8x-10} = 12$$
$$(-0.8x - 10)\log 2 = \log 12$$
$$-0.8x - 10 = \frac{\log 12}{\log 2}$$
$$-0.8x = \frac{\log 12}{\log 2} + 10$$
$$x = -\frac{1}{0.8}\left(\frac{\log 12}{\log 2} + 10\right) = -1.25\left(\frac{\log 12}{\log 2} + 10\right)$$

d. A reflection across both axes, a stretch horizontally by $\frac{5}{4}$, and a translation left by 12.5 units and up 12 units.

e. $(-12.5, 11)$

f. $f^{-1}(x) = -1.25\left(\dfrac{\log(-x + 12)}{\log 2} + 10\right)$

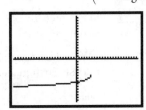

$[-47, 47, 2, -31, 31, 2]$

Note: The calculator graph does not show the graph approaching positive infinity to the left of the asymptote $x = 12$.

g. Domain: $x < 12$; range: All real numbers

h. Possible answer: $f^{-1}(f(x))$, or Y3, graphs as the entire line $y = x$. This is what we expect when we find the composition of a function with its inverse. $f(f^{-1}(x))$, or Y4, however, graphs to the line $y = x$, but it is only defined for domain values less than 12. This is because the domain of $f^{-1}(x)$ is only numbers less than 12. The graph of $f(f^{-1}(x))$ is a ray with endpoint $(12, 12)$ undefined.

3 Points
Parts a–f are correct and complete. Part g is attempted but not correct. Part h is attempted, but the explanation is not adequate.

1 Point
Parts a–c are correct and complete. The description of the transformations in part d is not correct. Part e is not correct because part d is incorrect. Part f is correct. Part g may not be correct, and part h has an inadequate explanation.

4. 5 Points
Answers are correct and complete. Explanations are clear, complete, and logical.

a. About 631 times. Possible method: Let I_{SF} and I_{NV} be the intensities of the San Francisco and Napa Valley earthquakes, respectively.

$$7.7 = \log \frac{I_{SF}}{I_0} \qquad 4.9 = \log \frac{I_{NV}}{I_0}$$

$$10^{7.7} = \frac{I_{SF}}{I_0} \qquad 10^{4.9} = \frac{I_{NV}}{I_0}$$

$$10^{7.7} I_0 = I_{SF} \qquad 10^{4.9} I_0 = I_{NV}$$

$$\frac{I_{SF}}{I_{NV}} = \frac{10^{7.7} I_0}{10^{4.9} I_0} = \frac{10^{7.7}}{10^{4.9}} \approx 631$$

b. About 9.5. Possible method: Let M_C be the magnitude of the Chile earthquake. The intensity of the Chile earthquake is $63 I_{SF}$, where I_{SF} is the intensity of the San Francisco earthquake.

$$M_C = \log \frac{63 I_{SF}}{I_0} \qquad \text{The magnitude formula.}$$

$$= \log \left(63 \cdot \frac{I_{SF}}{I_0} \right)$$

$$= \log 63 + \log \frac{I_{SF}}{I_0} \quad \text{Product property of logarithms.}$$

$$= \log 63 + 7.7 \qquad \log \frac{I_{SF}}{I_0} \text{ is the magnitude of the SF earthquake.}$$

$$\approx 9.5 \qquad \text{Evaluate.}$$

c. $10^{8.5}$, or 316,227,766 construction site blasts. Possible method: I need to find $\frac{I_C}{I_S}$, where I_C is the intensity of the Chile earthquake and I_S is the intensity of a construction site blast.

Using the magnitude formula,

$$\log \frac{I_C}{I_0} = 9.5 \qquad \log \frac{I_S}{I_0} = 1$$

$$\frac{I_C}{I_0} = 10^{9.5} \qquad \frac{I_S}{I_0} = 10^1$$

$$\frac{I_C}{I_S} = \frac{I_C}{I_0} \div \frac{I_S}{I_0} = \frac{10^{9.5}}{10^1} = 10^{8.5} = 316,227,766.$$

3 Points
The answer to part a is complete and correct. The answers to parts b and c are attempted, and one of the two answers is complete and correct.

1 Point
The answer to part a is correct. The other answers are incorrect.

CHAPTER 6 • Quiz 1

1. a.

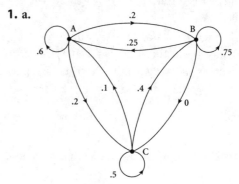

b.

	Second test		
	A	B	C
A	.6	.2	.2
B	.25	.75	0
C	.1	.4	.5

(First test — row labels A, B, C)

2. a. Not possible; The inner dimensions are not equal.

b. $\begin{bmatrix} 11 & -10 \\ -8 & 6 \end{bmatrix}$

c. $\begin{bmatrix} -5 & -40 & 10 & -5 & 0 \\ -15 & -25 & 0 & 20 & -30 \end{bmatrix}$

d. $[12 \quad -7]$

CHAPTER 6 • Quiz 2

1. a. $\begin{cases} 3x + 5y = 1790 \\ x = 2y - 100 \end{cases}$, where x is the number of student tickets sold and y is the number of nonstudent tickets sold.

b. 280 student tickets; 190 nonstudent tickets

2. $x = 4$, $y = -2$, $z = 3$. Work should be shown.

3. $(-3, 2, 4)$

CHAPTER 6 · Quiz 3

1. Vertices: $(-2, 2)$, $(2, 4)$, $(2, 1)$, $(0, 1)$

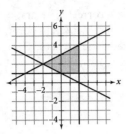

2. a. $(2, 4)$　　**b.** $(2, 1)$　　**c.** $(2, 1)$

3. 125 ft^2

CHAPTER 6 · Test

1. a. $[-12 \quad 0]$

b. $\begin{bmatrix} 2 & -2 \\ 11 & 0 \end{bmatrix}$

c. $\begin{bmatrix} 0 & 10 \\ -30 & 40 \\ 4 & -6 \end{bmatrix}$

d. Impossible; the inner dimensions are not the same.

e. $\begin{bmatrix} 7 & -6 \\ 24 & -3 \end{bmatrix}$

2. $(-5, 4)$

3. $(-1, 2.5, 3)$

4. a. Vertices: $(-1, 4)$, $(0, 4)$, $(4, 1)$, $(0.5, 1)$

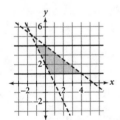

b. $(-1, 4)$

c. $(4, 1)$

5. a.

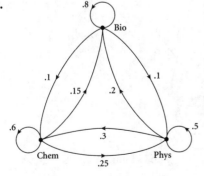

b.

	Next year		
	Bio	Chem	Phys
This year Bio	.8	.1	.1
Chem	.15	.6	.25
Phys	.2	.3	.5

c. 632; 550; 398

d. 691 biology majors; 494 chemistry majors; 395 physics majors

6. $\begin{cases} 2p + 4t + 5s = 30.75 \\ p + 3t + 3s = 17.50 \\ 5p + 7t + 12s = 71.75 \end{cases}$

Cheese pizza: \$9.25; topping: \$1.50; soft drink: \$1.25

CHAPTER 6 · Constructive Assessment Options

SCORING RUBRICS

1. 5 Points

Answers are correct and complete.

a. **i.** The total number of each type of car produced last week

ii. The total number of cars produced at each plant last week

iii. The total number of team hours last week in each plant on each assembly stage

b. **i.** $[B] \begin{bmatrix} 1 \\ 1 \\ 1 \end{bmatrix}$

ii. $[1 \quad 1 \quad 1][A][B]$

c. $[P] = \begin{bmatrix} 4000 \\ 3500 \\ 2800 \end{bmatrix}$; $[A][P]$

d. Two possible answers:

Method 1

Find $[P][1 \quad 1 \quad 1][A]$. The profits from each type of car will appear along the diagonal from the upper left to the lower right (a_{11} will be the profit from the Aries, a_{22} the profit from the Dinky, and a_{33} the profit from the Putter).

Method 2

Let $[Q] = \begin{bmatrix} 4000 & 4000 & 4000 \\ 3500 & 3500 & 3500 \\ 2800 & 2800 & 2800 \end{bmatrix}$

and find $[Q][A]$. The profits from each type of car will appear along the diagonal from the upper left to the lower right.

3 Points

The answer to four of the five subparts of parts a and b are correct. The answer to *either* part c *or* part d is correct.

1 Point

The answer to three of the five subparts of parts a and b are correct. The answers to parts c and d are incorrect.

2. 5 Points

Answers are correct and complete. Explanations are clear, complete, and logical.

a. Possible rule: Start with 4. To generate the remaining terms, add 2, then add 6, then add 10, then add 14, each time increasing the number added to the previous term by 4.

b. 36, 54, 76

c. $u_1 = 4$ and $u_n = u_{n-1} + 2 + 4(n - 2)$ where $n \geq 2$, or $u_1 = 4$ and $u_n = u_{n-1} + 4n - 6$ where $n \geq 2$.

d. $a = 2$, $b = -4$, $c = 6$. Possible method: Using the fact that $f(1) = 4$, $f(2) = 6$, and $f(3) = 12$, write a system of equations.

$$\begin{cases} a + b + c = 4 \\ 4a + 2b + c = 6 \\ 9a + 3b + c = 12 \end{cases}$$

Write the system as $[A][X] = [B]$, where

$$[A] = \begin{bmatrix} 1 & 1 & 1 \\ 4 & 2 & 1 \\ 9 & 3 & 1 \end{bmatrix} \text{ and } [B] = \begin{bmatrix} 4 \\ 6 \\ 12 \end{bmatrix}.$$

Use a calculator to find

$$[X] = [A]^{-1}[B] = \begin{bmatrix} 2 \\ -4 \\ 6 \end{bmatrix}.$$

Therefore $a = 2$, $b = -4$, and $c = 6$.

3 Points

The answers to parts a, b, and d are complete and correct. The answer to part c is incorrect or missing.

1 Point

The answers to parts a and b are correct. The other answers are incorrect or missing.

3. 5 Points

Answers are correct and complete.

a. $6w + 5g \leq 420$ **b.** $9w + 15g \leq 780$

c. $\dfrac{w}{g} \geq \dfrac{3}{7}$, or $7w \geq 3g$ **d.** $w \geq 0$, $g \geq 0$

e. The vertices are $A(0, 0)$, $B(70, 0)$, $C\left(53\frac{1}{3}, 20\right)$, $D\left(17\frac{8}{11}, 41\frac{4}{11}\right)$.

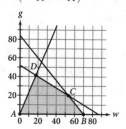

f. $P = 3.50w + 6.50g$; 18 widgets and 41 gizmos; $329.50

3 Points

The answers to parts a–d are correct. The graph in part e is essentially correct, but incorrect coordinates may be given for one of the vertices. The answer to part f is incorrect or missing.

1 Point

The answers to parts a–d are mostly correct. The answers to parts e and f are incorrect or missing.

CHAPTERS 4–6 · Exam

1. a. $f(-3) = 3$

    b. $x = -\dfrac{2}{3}$, $x = -3$, and $1 \leq x \leq 2$

    c. Domain: $-3 \leq x \leq 3$; range: $-1 \leq y \leq 4$

    d.

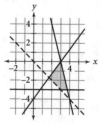

    e. No; possible explanation: The graph does not pass the vertical line test.

2. a. 1.45   **b.** 3.29   **c.** 19

    d. 130   **e.** 1000

3. a. $-27x^9$ **b.** $3.125x^{-1}$ **c.** $4x^{5/3}$

4. $\begin{bmatrix} 6 & 4 \\ -4 & 9 \\ 31 & 16 \end{bmatrix}$

5. a. $y = -(x - 3)^2 + 2$

    b. $y = |2x| - 1$, or $y = 2|x| - 1$

    c. $\left(\dfrac{x}{3}\right)^2 + \left(\dfrac{y - 3}{2}\right)^2 = 1$, or $y = 3 \pm 2\sqrt{1 - \left(\dfrac{x}{3}\right)^2}$

6. Skippy: 16 pounds; Gizmo: 52 pounds; Chopper: 98 pounds

7. a. Vertices: $(3, 0)$, $\left(\dfrac{12}{7}, -\dfrac{12}{7}\right)$, $(3, -3)$, $\left(\dfrac{15}{4}, -3\right)$

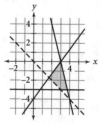

    b. $(3, -3)$

8. a. 5%   **b.** $3500   **c.** 23 years

CHAPTER 7 · Quiz 1

1. $y = 2x^2 - 5x - 4$

2. a. $x = 2$ and $x = -11$ **b.** $x = 0$ and $x = 0.25$

  c. $x = 0$ and $x = 5$

3. Vertex form: $y = (x + 2)^2 - 9$; factored form:
$y = (x + 5)(x - 1)$

4. a. $y = (x + 6)^2 - 1$; vertex $(-6, -1)$

  b. $y = -5(x + 2)^2 + 32$; vertex $(-2, 32)$

CHAPTER 7 · Quiz 2

1. 6.90 s

2. a. $3 + 3i$ **b.** $8 + 5i$

3. a. $-\frac{1}{2} + \frac{5}{2}i$ **b.** 34

4. a. $x = \pm i\sqrt{8}$ $\left(\text{or } x = \pm 2i\sqrt{2}\right)$

  b. $x = \dfrac{-4 \pm \sqrt{8}}{2}$ $\left(\text{or } x = -2 \pm \sqrt{2}\right)$

CHAPTER 7 · Quiz 3

1. Possible answer: $y = -4(x + 2)(x - 2)(x - 6)$

2. Possible answer: $y = x^3 - 6x^2 + 18x - 40$

3. $x = -\frac{5}{7}$, $x = \sqrt{7}$, and $x = -\sqrt{7}$

4. $y = 0.5(x - 3)(x + 5)^2$

CHAPTER 7 · Test

1. a. $x = -5$ or $x = 3$

  b. $x = 0$, $x = -2$, or $x = -4$

2. a. Vertex form; general form: $y = 5x^2 - 20x + 17$;
factored form:

$$y = 5\left(x - \left(2 + \frac{\sqrt{15}}{5}\right)\right)\left(x - \left(2 - \frac{\sqrt{15}}{5}\right)\right)$$

  b. Factored form; general form: $y = -3x^2 +$
$21x - 36$; vertex form: $y = -3\left(x - \frac{7}{2}\right)^2 + \frac{3}{4}$

  c. General form; vertex form: $y = (x - 2)^2 + 2$;
factored form:

$$y = \left(x - \left(2 + i\sqrt{2}\right)\right)\left(x - \left(2 - i\sqrt{2}\right)\right)$$

3. a. $y = 2x(x - 3)(x + 3)$

  b. $y = -0.25(x + 4)(x + 2)(x - 2)^2$

4. a.

Side length	1	2	3	4	5
Number of squares	1	5	14	30	55

  b. 91

  c. 3

5. a. $\pm 1, \pm 2, \pm 4, \pm 8, \pm 16, \pm\frac{1}{3}, \pm\frac{2}{3}, \pm\frac{4}{3}, \pm\frac{8}{3}, \pm\frac{16}{3}$

  b. -2 and $\frac{4}{3}$

  c. $1 + i$ and $1 - i$

  d. $P(x) =$

$$3(x + 2)\left(x - \frac{4}{3}\right)(x - (1 + i))(x - (1 - i))$$

6. a. 5.21 s

  b. 2.86 s

  c. 70.00 m; 1.43 s

7. $y = 2.5x^4 + 42.5x^2 + 40$

8. As x takes on larger negative values, y becomes
increasingly negative. As x takes on larger positive
values, y becomes increasingly negative. The
x-intercepts are -5, -2, 0, and 2. The y-intercept
is 0. There are local maximums at about
$(-3.9, 48.1)$ and $(1.2, 19.1)$ and a local
minimum at about $(-1.0, -12.0)$.

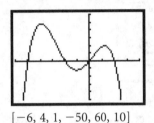

$[-6, 4, 1, -50, 60, 10]$

CHAPTER 7 · Constructive Assessment Options

SCORING RUBRICS

1. 5 Points
Answers are correct and complete. Explanations are
clear, complete, and logical.

  a.

Time (s)	0.5	1.0	1.5	2.0	2.5	3.0
Distance (m)	1.23	4.90	11.03	19.60	30.63	44.10

D_1 3.67   6.13   8.57   11.03   13.47

D_2 2.46   2.44   2.46   2.44

The second differences are nearly constant, so the
data can be modeled by a quadratic function of
the form $d(t) = at^2 + bt + c$.

  b. Answers will vary, but students should choose
consecutive values. Using the first three data
values gives the system

$$\begin{cases} 0.25a + 0.5b + c = 1.23 \\ a + b + c = 4.90 \\ 2.25a + 1.5b + c = 11.03 \end{cases}$$

The solution is $a = 4.92$, $b = -0.04$, and
$c = 0.02$. Therefore, the model is $d(t) =$
$4.92t^2 - 0.04t + 0.02$.

c. Answers will vary. Using the data points (1.0, 4.9), (2.0, 19.60), and (3.0, 44.10) gives the system

$$\begin{cases} a + b + c = 4.9 \\ 4a + 2b + c = 19.6 \\ 9a + 3b + c = 44.10 \end{cases}$$

The solution is $a = 4.9$, $b = 0$, and $c = 0$, so the model is $d(t) = 4.9t^2$.

d. Answers will vary, but choice should be supported by sound reasoning. Possible answer: I think $d(t) = 4.9t^2$ is a better model. In general, it is better to use data values that are spread out when finding a model. Graphs suggest that both models fit the data very well. In the table below, L3 shows the differences between the data values and the function values for the first model, and L4 shows the differences between the data values and the function values for the second model.

L2	L3	L4	5
1.23	0	-.005	
4.9	0	0	
11.03	0	-.005	
19.6	.02	0	
30.63	.04	-.005	
44.1	.08	0	
------	-----	------	
L4(6) =0			

In the first model, the differences increase as t increases. In the second model, the differences for the three points that were not used to find the model are all the same, small value, -0.005. This suggests that $d(t) = 4.9t^2$ is a better model. Based on this evidence and the fact that $d(t) = 4.9t^2$ is simpler and easier to use than the other model, I would choose $d(t) = 4.9t^2$.

3 Points
The answers to parts a–c are complete and correct. Part d is attempted, but the reasoning is weak or illogical.

1 Point
The answers to part a is correct. One of the models in parts b and c is correct. Part d is not attempted.

2. 5 Points
Answers are correct, and explanations are clear, complete, and logical.

a. $h(0) = 1.3$; the ball is at a height of 1.3 m when the center fielder releases it.

b. About 4.15 s. Possible explanation: When the ball reaches the plate, its height is 0. To find the time when this happens, solve $-4.9t^2 + 20t + 1.3 = 0$. Using the quadratic formula,

$$t = \frac{-20 \pm \sqrt{20^2 - 4(-4.9)(1.3)}}{2(-4.9)} = \frac{-20 \pm \sqrt{425.48}}{-9.8}$$

Simplifying gives $t \approx -0.064$ and $t \approx 4.15$. Only the positive answer makes sense. So the ball reaches the plate about 4.15 s after it is thrown.

c. About 21.71 m; about 2.04 s. Possible explanation: The t-value of the maximum height occurs midway between the zeros, or at about $t = 2.04$. To find the maximum height, substitute 2.04 for t in the equation: $h(2.04) = -4.9(2.04)^2 + 20(2.04) + 1.3 \approx 21.71$.

d. 7.52 m/s. Possible explanation: It took the ball 4.15 s to reach home plate. Because the runner hesitated for half a second before running, it took him $4.15 - 0.5$, or 3.65, s to run the 90 ft to home plate. Convert 90 ft to meters: 90 ft = 1080 in. = 2743.2 cm = 27.432 m. The runner's speed in meters per second is $\frac{27.432 \text{ m}}{3.65 \text{ s}} \approx$ 7.52 m/s.

e. No. Possible explanation: The graph does not show the path of the ball. The variable on the horizontal axis is time, not the horizontal distance covered by the ball.

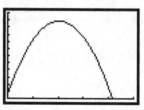

[0, 5, 1, 0, 24, 2]

3 Points
The answers to parts a–c include one minor error. The answer to part d is incorrect or unclear. The graph in part e may be correct, but the explanation is incorrect or missing.

1 Point
Two of the answers in parts a–c are incorrect. The answers to parts d and e are incorrect or missing.

3. 5 Points
Answers are correct and complete. Explanations are clear, complete, and logical.

a. x by $(24 - 2x)$ by $(30 - 2x)$ units

b. Factored form: $V(x) = x(24 - 2x)(30 - 2x)$, or $V(x) = 4x(x - 12)(x - 15)$; general form: $V(x) = 4x^3 - 108x^2 + 720x$

c. $0 < x < 12$. Possible explanation: Negative values of x don't make sense because x is a length. If x were 0, then no cuts or folds would be made and no box would be formed. If x were 12, then the width would be 0, so no box would exist. If x were greater than 12, then the width would be negative, which doesn't make sense.

d. About 1418 units^3; answers may vary slightly due to tracing.

e. 1.884 by 20.231 by 26.231 units and 7.555 by 8.889 by 14.889 units

f. x by $(a - 2x)$ by $\left(\frac{b}{2} - 2x\right)$ units; factored form: $V(x) = x(a - 2x)\left(\frac{b}{2} - 2x\right)$; general form: $V(x) = 4x^3 - 2\left(a + \frac{b}{2}\right)x^2 + \frac{abx}{2}$

g. $0 < x < \frac{a}{2}$. Possible explanation: Negative values of x don't make sense because x is a length. If x were 0, then no cuts would be made and no box would be formed. If x were $\frac{a}{2}$, then the length and width would be 0, so no box would exist. If x were greater than $\frac{a}{2}$, then the length and width would be negative, which doesn't make sense.

3 Points
The answers to four parts are correct. The other answers are attempted and some correct work is shown.

1 Point
The answers to two parts are correct. The other answers are missing or incorrect.

4. 5 Points
Answers are correct and complete. Explanations are clear, complete, and logical.

a. $z = 9$; -3 and 3   **b.** $z = -25$; $-5i$ and $5i$

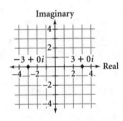 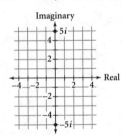

c. $z = 8$; 2, $-1 + i\sqrt{3}$, and $-1 - i\sqrt{3}$

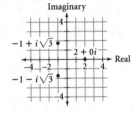

d. $z = -1$; -1, $\frac{1}{2} + \frac{\sqrt{3}}{2}i$, and $\frac{1}{2} - \frac{\sqrt{3}}{2}i$

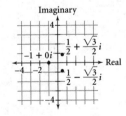

e. $z = -4$; $1 + i$, $1 - i$, $-1 + i$, $-1 - i$

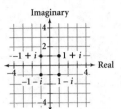

f. $z = 16$; 2, -2, $2i$, $-2i$

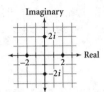

g. The answer should include at least two of the following observations:

- The number of roots of z is equal to the power the number was raised to (or, in each case, there were n nth roots).

- The roots are evenly distributed around a circle with center at the origin.

- The angle between the roots is 360° divided by the number of roots.

3 Points
In parts a–f, all the values of z are correct. Of the 18 roots found, 3 or 4 are missing or incorrect. The graphs match the roots found. The answer to part g includes only one correct observation.

1 Point
In parts a–f, at least four values of z are correct. Of the 18 roots found, 8 or 9 are missing. The graphs match the roots found. The answer to part g is missing or includes no correct observations.

CHAPTER 8 · Quiz 1

1. a.   **b.**

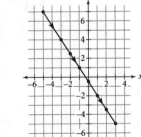 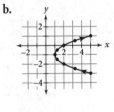

2. a. $y = -\frac{3}{2}x - \frac{1}{2}$ **b.** $y = -1 \pm \sqrt{x - 1}$

3. a. Possible answer: $x = t$, $y = |t|$

    b. Possible answer: $x = t - 3$, $y = 2|t|$

CHAPTER 8 · Quiz 2

1. 9.6

2. About 56°

3. a. 9.5 hours

   b. 207 miles west, 96 miles south

4. About 34°

5. a. 5.5 ft; 29°   **b.** 72 ft/s

   c. The height of the projectile is about 21.9 ft, and it is at a horizontal distance of about 94.5 ft from where it was released.

CHAPTER 8 · Quiz 3

1. $m \approx 19.6$, $n \approx 8.9$

2. $m\angle D \approx 89°$, $m\angle F \approx 51°$, $m\angle F \approx 40°$ (*Note:* Answers may vary by 1°, depending on how students found the measures.)

3. 9.0 miles

CHAPTER 8 · Test

1. a.   **b.** $y = 2x^2 - 2$

   c. The graph in part a is the part of the graph below for $0 \le x \le \sqrt{2.5}$. Possible explanation: The parametric equation $x = \sqrt{0.5t}$ only gives x-values greater than or equal to 0, so the parametric graph does not include negative x-values. Because $t \le 5$, the parametric graph only goes to $\sqrt{2.5}$.

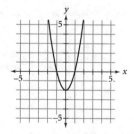

2. a. Possible answer: $x = t$, $y = t^2 - 4$

   b. Possible answer: $x = t$, $y = -(t^2 - 4)$

   c. Possible answer: $x = 2t$, $y = t^2 - 4$

   d. Possible answer: $x = -(t + 2)$, $y = t^2 - 4$

3. a. 7.2   **b.** 11.0   **c.** 70°   **d.** 24°

4. a. Yes. It passes about 4 ft above the crossbar.

   b. About 146 ft, or 49 yd

5. a. Ship A: $x = 22t \cos 35°$, $y = 22t \sin 35°$; ship B: $x = 19t \cos 170°$, $y = 19t \sin 170°$

   b. 107 miles; 78 miles west and 14 miles north of Seaside

   c. 227 miles

6. 174.87°

CHAPTER 8 · Constructive Assessment Options

SCORING RUBRICS

1. 5 Points
Answers are correct and complete. Explanations are clear, complete, and logical.

   a.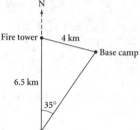

   b. About 6.8 km or about 3.9 km. Possible explanation: Let x represent the measure of the angle with vertex at the base camp, and use the Law of Sines.

$$\frac{\sin 35°}{4} = \frac{\sin x}{6.5}$$

$$\sin x = \frac{6.5 \sin 35°}{4}$$

$$x = \sin^{-1}\left(\frac{6.5 \sin 35°}{4}\right) \approx 69°$$

This is the ambiguous case, so it is also possible that x is equal to the supplement of 69°, or 111°. Use the Law of Sines to find the distance, d, to the base camp in each case.

Discovering Advanced Algebra Assessment Resources B
©2004 Key Curriculum Press

If $x = 69°$, then the angle with the fire tower as its vertex has measure $180° - (69° + 35°) = 76°$. So

$$\frac{\sin 35°}{4} = \frac{\sin 76°}{d}$$

$$d = \frac{4 \sin 76°}{\sin 35°} \approx 6.8$$

If $x = 111°$, then the angle with the fire tower as its vertex has measure $180° - (111° + 35°) = 34°$. So

$$\frac{\sin 35°}{4} = \frac{\sin 34°}{d}$$

$$d = \frac{4 \sin 34°}{\sin 35°} \approx 3.9$$

So Sharon and Wanda are either about 6.8 km or about 3.9 km from the base camp.

c. If they could recall their bearing as they hiked from the base camp to the fire tower, they would know which of the possibilities given in part b is correct.

d. Estimates and explanations should be logical and based on information from the problem. Possible answer: If they have 6.8 km to go, it will take them about 3.4 hours, or 3 hours 24 minutes, to get to base camp. If they have 3.9 km to go, it will take them about 1.95 hours, or 1 hour 57 minutes. If they are not able to remember the information in part c, they could assume that they are 6.8 km away and predict that they will arrive at 4:24 P.M. If they are correct, they will get 50 bonus points. If they are really only 3.9 km away, they will arrive at about 2:57 P.M. and get 100 bonus points. On the other hand, they could predict that they will arrive at 2:57 P.M. In this case, if they really are only 3.9 km away, they get 150 bonus points. If they are wrong, they get no bonus points. The decision might depend on how much they are willing to gamble or perhaps on how many bonus points they need to be assured of a victory. (If they need 150 bonus points to win, they might as well gamble.)

3 Points
The answers to parts a–c are complete and correct. The answer to part d is unclear, incorrect, or missing.

1 Point
The diagram in part a is correct. Only one possible distance is given in part b. Part d is clear and logical based on the answer to part b. The answer to part c may or may not be correct.

2. 5 Points
Answers are correct and complete. Explanations are clear, complete, and logical.

a. About 4.55 m, 9.10 m, and 6.35 m. Possible explanation: Let x be the length of one side of the pen. The lengths of the other sides are $2x$ and $20 - 3x$.

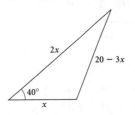

Use the Law of Cosines to write an equation for x and the quadratic formula to solve it.

$$(20 - 3x)^2 = x^2 + (2x)^2 - 2(x)(2x) \cos 40°$$

$$400 - 120x + 9x^2 = x^2 + 4x^2 - 4x^2 \cos 40°$$

$$4x^2 \cos 40° + 4x^2 - 120x + 400 = 0$$

$$7.064x^2 - 120x + 400 = 0$$

$$x \approx 4.55 \text{ or } x \approx 12.43$$

If $x \approx 12.43$, then the perimeter would be greater than 20. Therefore, $x \approx 4.55$. The side lengths are about 4.55 m, 9.10 m, and 6.35 m.

b. About 13.3 m². Possible explanation: Let h be the length of the altitude to the 9.10 m side.

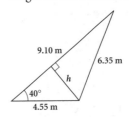

Then $h = 4.55 \sin 40° \approx 2.92$ m. Now use the formula for the area of a triangle, $A = \frac{1}{2}bh$.

$$A \approx \frac{1}{2}(9.10)(2.92) \approx 13.3$$

The area is about 13.3 m².

3 Points
A correct procedure is used for part a, but an algebraic error leads to the incorrect answer. The correct procedure is used for part b, but the answer is incorrect because it is based on the incorrect answer from part a.

1 Point
A correct procedure is used for part a, but an algebraic error leads to the incorrect answer. Part b is not attempted.

3. 5 Points
Answers are correct and complete. Explanations are clear, complete, and logical.

a. $x = 70t \cos \theta$, $y = -16t^2 + 70t \sin \theta + 5$. (*Note:* These equations are in feet and seconds.)

b.

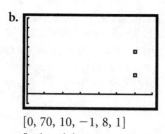

[0, 70, 10, −1, 8, 1]
$0 \leq t \leq 1$

c. Possible answer: $8.6° \leq \theta \leq 11.0°$

d. Possible answer: $4.0° \leq \theta \leq 6.4°$

e. Possible answer: For both pitches, the range of angles that will result in a strike is very small. The pitcher must have great control. The range for both pitches is the same, so the level of control needed is the same regardless of the speed of the pitch.

3 Points
The answers to parts a–d include one minor error. Part e is attempted, but the answer is unclear or incorrect.

1 Point
The answers to parts a and b are correct. The answers to parts c–e are incorrect or missing.

CHAPTER 9 · Quiz 1

1. $y = \frac{1}{8}x - \frac{19}{16}$

2. $(x + 3)^2 + (y - 4)^2 = 8$; $x = -3 + \sqrt{8} \cos t$, $y = 4 + \sqrt{8} \sin t$

3. $\left(\frac{x - 2}{3}\right)^2 + \left(\frac{y - 3}{2}\right)^2 = 1$; $(2 + \sqrt{5}, 3)$, $(2 - \sqrt{5}, 3)$

CHAPTER 9 · Quiz 2

1. $(y + 3)^2 = -4(x - 3)$

2. $(3 - \sqrt{5}, 0)$, $(3 + \sqrt{5}, 0)$

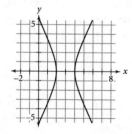

3. $\left(\frac{x + 2}{4}\right)^2 + \left(\frac{y - 5}{3}\right)^2 = 1$; an ellipse with center $(-2, 5)$, a horizontal major axis of length 8, and a vertical minor axis of length 6

4. $\frac{(x - 1)^2}{-2} = y - 2$

CHAPTER 9 · Quiz 3

1. The parent function was stretched vertically by a factor of 3 and then translated right 7 units and up 5 units.

2. Hole at $x = 5$; vertical asymptote $x = -2$, horizontal asymptote $y = 2$; x-intercept 0, y-intercept 0

3. $\frac{x^2 + 6x - 17}{(x + 2)(x - 3)^2}$

4. $\frac{x + 1}{2(x - 5)}$, $x \neq 2$, $x \neq 5$

CHAPTER 9 · Test

1. $\left(\frac{x + 4}{2}\right)^2 + \left(\frac{y - 3}{2}\right)^2 = 1$

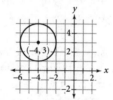

2. $\left(\frac{y}{3}\right)^2 - \left(\frac{x + 3}{2}\right)^2 = 1$

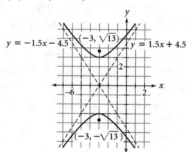

3. $y = -\frac{(x - 1)^2}{5}$

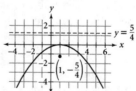

4. 108 mL

5. $\left(\frac{x + 2}{4}\right)^2 + \left(\frac{y + 2}{5}\right)^2 = 1$

6. $y = \frac{(x - 3)^2}{8} - 1$

7. $\frac{(y - 1)^2}{4} - (x + 3)^2 = 1$

Discovering Advanced Algebra Assessment Resources B
©2004 Key Curriculum Press

8.

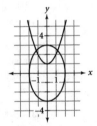

9. Vertical asymptote at $x = -5$, horizontal asymptote at $y = 1$, x-intercepts at $(-2, 0)$ and $(5, 0)$, y-intercept at $(0, -0.4)$

10. a. $\dfrac{-2x + 13}{(x + 5)(x - 3)(x + 4)}$

   b. $\dfrac{x + 1}{x - 2}$, $x \neq -8$, $x \neq 4$

CHAPTER 9 · Constructive Assessment Options

SCORING RUBRICS

1. 5 Points

Answers are correct and complete. Explanations are clear, complete, and logical.

   a. Possible descriptions: $x^2 - y + 1 = 0$ is the equation of a parabola congruent to the parent parabola $y = x^2$ translated up 1 unit. $9x^2 + 4y^2 - 36 = 0$ is the equation of an ellipse with center $(0, 0)$, a vertical major axis of length 6, and a horizontal minor axis of length 4.

   b. They appear to have two points of intersection.

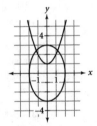

   c. About $(-1.19, 2.41)$ and $(1.19, 2.41)$. Possible explanation: Solve $x^2 - y + 1 = 0$ for x^2 to get $x^2 = y - 1$. Substitute $y - 1$ for x^2 in $9x^2 + 4y^2 - 36 = 0$ and solve for y.

$$9(y - 1) + 4y^2 - 36 = 0$$
$$9y - 9 + 4y^2 - 36 = 0$$
$$4y^2 + 9y - 45 = 0$$
$$y = \frac{-9 \pm \sqrt{9^2 - 4(4)(-45)}}{2(4)}$$
$$y \approx 2.41 \text{ or } y \approx -4.66$$

Substitute each value into $x^2 = y - 1$ and solve for x.

$$x^2 \approx 2.41 - 1 \qquad x^2 \approx -4.66 - 1$$
$$x \approx \pm 1.19 \qquad x \text{ is nonreal}$$

So the points of intersection are about $(-1.19, 2.41)$ and $(1.19, 2.41)$.

---

   d. $x = t$, $y = t^2 + 1$ and $x = 2 \cos t$, $y = 3 \sin t$; tracing the graph shows that the intersections points found in part c are correct.

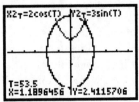

$[-5.5, 5.5, 1, -3.5, 3.5, 1]$
$0 \leq t \leq 360$

3 Points

The answers to parts a and b are complete and correct. The procedure used in part c is correct and is clearly described, but the intersection points are incorrect owing to a computation error. The parametric equations in part d are correct, but it is not clear that the intersection points were checked.

1 Point

The answer to parts a and b are essentially correct. The answers to parts c and d are missing or include significant errors.

2. 5 Points

Answers are correct and complete. Explanations are clear, complete, and logical.

   a. $y = \frac{1}{4}(x - 2)^2 + 3$; 4 units. Possible explanation: The vertex is $(2, 3)$. The directed distance from the vertex to the focus, f, is 1. The equation is therefore $(y - 3) = 4(x - 2)^2$, or $y = \frac{1}{4}(x - 2)^2 + 3$. The y-coordinate of both endpoints of the chord is 4, the same as the y-coordinate of the focus. To find the x-coordinates, substitute 4 for y in the equation of the parabola and solve for x.

$$4 = \frac{1}{4}(x - 2)^2 + 3$$
$$1 = \frac{1}{4}(x - 2)^2$$
$$4 = (x - 2)^2$$
$$x - 2 = \pm 2$$
$$x = 2 \pm 2$$
$$x = 0 \text{ or } x = 4$$

The endpoints of the chord are $(0, 4)$ and $(4, 4)$. The distance between these points is 4 units, so the width of the parabola is 4.

   b. $y = \frac{1}{16}(x - 2)^2$; 16 units

   c. $y = \frac{1}{2(b - c)}(x - a)^2 + \frac{b + c}{2}$; $2|b - c|$ units.

   Possible explanation: The vertex is $\left(a, \frac{b + c}{2}\right)$.

   The directed distance from the vertex to

the focus, f, is $\frac{b-c}{2}$. The equation is

$$y = \frac{1}{4 \cdot \frac{b-c}{2}}(x-a)^2 + \frac{b+c}{2}, \text{ or}$$

$$y = \frac{1}{2(b-c)}(x-a)^2 + \frac{b+c}{2}.$$

The y-coordinate of both endpoints of the chord is b, the same as the y-coordinate of the focus. To find the x-coordinates, substitute b for y in the equation of the parabola and solve for x.

$$b = \frac{1}{2(b-c)}(x-a)^2 + \frac{b+c}{2}$$

$$\frac{b-c}{2} = \frac{1}{2(b-c)}(x-a)^2$$

$$(b-c)^2 = (x-a)^2$$

$$x - a = \pm(b-c)$$

$$x = a \pm (b-c)$$

So the endpoints of the chord are $(a+b-c, b)$ and $(a-b+c, b)$. The width is $|(a+b-c) - (a-b+c)|$, or $2|b-c|$ units.

d. Conjectures should be based on the work in parts a–c. Possible conjecture: The width of a parabola is twice the distance from the focus to the directrix.

3 Points
The answers to parts a and b are complete and correct. The method used in part c is correct, but the equation and/or the length are wrong owing to an algebraic error. The conjecture in part d is missing or incorrect.

1 Point
Of the four answers in parts a and b (two equations and two lengths), two are correct. The answers to parts c and d are missing or incorrect.

3. 5 Points
Answers are correct and complete. Explanations are clear, complete, and logical.

a. 10.9 Ω. Sample work:

$$\frac{1}{R_T} = \frac{1}{24} + \frac{1}{30} + \frac{1}{60} \qquad \text{Substitute the known values for } R_1, R_2, \text{ and } R_3.$$

$$\frac{1}{R_T} = \frac{5}{120} + \frac{4}{120} + \frac{2}{120} \qquad \text{Rewrite the fractions on the right with a common denominator.}$$

$$\frac{1}{R_T} = \frac{11}{120} \qquad \text{Add.}$$

$$R_T = \frac{120}{11} \approx 10.9 \qquad \text{Find the reciprocal of both sides.}$$

b. 128 Ω. Sample work:

$$\frac{1}{32} = \frac{1}{64} + \frac{1}{R_2} + \frac{1}{R_2} \qquad \text{Substitute the known values.}$$

$$\frac{1}{32} = \frac{R_2}{64R_2} + \frac{64}{64R_2} + \frac{64}{64R_2} \qquad \text{Rewrite the fractions on the right with a common denominator.}$$

$$\frac{1}{32} = \frac{128 + R_2}{64R_2} \qquad \text{Add.}$$

$$2R_2 = 128 + R_2 \qquad \text{Multiply both sides by } 64R_2.$$

$$R_2 = 128 \qquad \text{Solve for } R_2.$$

c. $R_1 \approx 84.66$ Ω, $R_2 \approx 42.33$ Ω, $R_3 \approx 68.66$ Ω. Sample work:

$$\frac{1}{20} = \frac{1}{2R_2} + \frac{1}{R_2} + \frac{1}{2R_2 - 16} \qquad \text{Substitute the known information.}$$

$$\frac{1}{20} = \frac{R_2 - 8}{2R_2(R_2 - 8)} + \frac{2(R_2 - 8)}{2R_2(R_2 - 8)} + \frac{R_2}{2R_2(R_2 - 8)} \qquad \text{Rewrite the fractions on the right with a common denominator.}$$

$$\frac{1}{20} = \frac{R_2 - 8 + 2R_2 - 16 + R_2}{2R_2(R_2 - 8)} \qquad \text{Add.}$$

$$\frac{1}{20} = \frac{4R_2 - 24}{2R_2(R_2 - 8)} \qquad \text{Collect like terms and add.}$$

$$\frac{1}{20} = \frac{2(R_2 - 6)}{R_2(R_2 - 8)} \qquad \text{Factor the numerator and reduce the fraction.}$$

$$R_2^2 - 8R_2 = 40R_2 - 240 \qquad \text{Multiply both sides by the common denominator and simplify.}$$

$$R_2^2 - 48R_2 + 240 = 0 \qquad \text{Write in general form.}$$

$$R_2 \approx 42.33 \text{ or } R_2 \approx 5.67 \qquad \text{Solve using the quadratic formula.}$$

If $R_2 \approx 5.67$ Ω, then R_3 would be negative, so $R_2 \approx 42.33$ Ω. Then $R_1 \approx 2(42.33) \approx 84.66$ Ω, and $R_3 \approx 84.66 - 16 \approx 68.66$ Ω.

d. Answer will depend on which resistance is used for the independent variable. If R_2 is used, the function is $R_T = \frac{R_2(R_2 - 8)}{2(R_2 - 6)}$, $R_2 > 8$. (Note that

Discovering Advanced Algebra Assessment Resources B
©2004 Key Curriculum Press

$R_3 = 2R_2 - 16 > 0$, so $R_2 > 8$. This also ensures that $R_1 \neq 0$, $R_2 \neq 0$, and $R_2 \neq 6$, so R_T is defined in all possible cases.)

e.

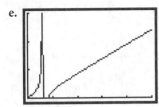

[0, 50, 10, 0, 30, 10]

f. The intersection points are about (42, 20) and (5.7, 20).

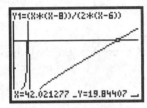

[0, 50, 10, 0, 30, 10]

g. The intersection (42, 20) confirms the answer in part c. The other intersection, (5.7, 20), has $R_2 = 5.7\ \Omega$. For this value of R_2, $R_3 = 2(5.7) - 16 = -4.6\ \Omega$. In the real world, a resistor cannot have negative resistance.

3 Points
The answers to parts a–c are complete and correct. Part d is attempted, but the answer is not correct. Parts e and f are consistent with the answer to part d. Part g does not check.

1 Point
Two of the three answers in parts a–c are complete and correct. Part d is attempted, but the answer is not correct. The answers to parts e–g are missing.

4. 5 Points
Answers are correct and complete. Explanations are clear, complete, and logical.

a. $-2, 2$

b. $x = -3$ and $x = 1$

c. $y = -2$

d.

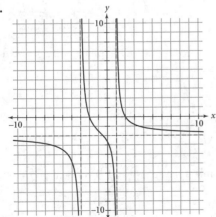

e. Domain: $-\infty < x < -3$, $-3 < x < 1$, and $1 < x < \infty$ (or, all real numbers except -3 and 1); range: all real numbers

f. $f(x)$ is positive for $-3 < x < -2$ and $1 < x < 2$; $f(x)$ is negative for $-\infty < x < -3$, $-2 < x < 1$, and $2 < x < \infty$.

g. $f(x)$ is never increasing; $f(x)$ is decreasing for $-\infty < x < -3$, $-3 < x < 1$, and $1 < x < \infty$.

3 Points
Of the 12 answers in parts a–g (2 intercepts, 3 asymptotes, 1 sketch, 1 domain, 1 range, 4 intervals), 8 are correct.

1 Point
Of the 12 answers in parts a–g, 3 are correct.

CHAPTERS 7–9 · Exam

1. a. $y + 2 = \left(\dfrac{x - 7}{\sqrt{3}}\right)^2$; parabola

b. $\left(\dfrac{x - 2}{5}\right)^2 + \left(\dfrac{y}{4}\right)^2 = 1$; ellipse

c. $\left(\dfrac{y + 5}{\sqrt{11}}\right)^2 - \left(\dfrac{x - 2}{3}\right)^2 = 1$; hyperbola

d. $\left(\dfrac{x - 6}{\sqrt{21}}\right)^2 + \left(\dfrac{y - 1}{\sqrt{21}}\right)^2 = 1$; circle

2. a. $13 - 6i$ **b.** $-\dfrac{39}{41} - \dfrac{23}{41}i$

c. $48 - 14i$ **d.** $-18 - 15i$

3. $y = \dfrac{1}{5}x^3 - x^2 + \dfrac{9}{5}x - 9$

4. a. Vertex: (2, 7); zeros: $2 \pm \dfrac{\sqrt{35}}{5}i$; minimum

b. Vertex: $(-5.5, 134.75)$; zeros: $-2, -9$; maximum

c. Vertex: (4, 0); zero: 4; minimum

5. a. $100.3°$ **b.** 2.4   **c.** 7.3

6. a. Ship A: $x = 21t\cos 30°$, $y = 21t\sin 30°$; ship B: $x = 24t\cos 45°$, $y = 120 - 24t\sin 45°$

b. 84 miles; about 103 miles

c. About 155 miles

7. a. 93 ft/s; $25°$; 6 ft

b. About (84, 29); that is, at a horizontal distance of 84 ft from where it was released and 29 ft from the ground

c. About 219 ft; about 2.60 s

8. a.

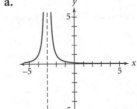

b.

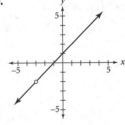

c.

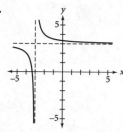

9. a. $\dfrac{x - 4}{(x + 4)(x - 6)}, x \neq 3$

b. $\dfrac{2(x + 2)}{x + 1}, x \neq -7, x \neq -3, x \neq 2$

10. a. $x^2 - \left(\dfrac{y + 3}{2}\right)^2 = 1$

b. $\left(\dfrac{x}{5}\right)^2 + \left(\dfrac{y - 4}{3}\right)^2 = 1$

11. $y = (x + 6)(x - 5)(x + 5)$

12. $(-1.27, -1.54), (0.47, 1.94)$

CHAPTER 10 · Quiz 1

1. a. $-\dfrac{1}{2}$ **b.** $-\dfrac{\sqrt{2}}{2}$

2. a. $80°$ **b.** $333°$

3. $41°$ and $319°$

4. $18°$ and $162°$

5. $\dfrac{16\pi}{9}$

6. $165°$

7. $\dfrac{10\pi}{3}$ cm

CHAPTER 10 · Quiz 2

1. a. Possible answer: $y = -\dfrac{1}{2}\cos x$

b. Possible answer: $y = 1 + \sin\left(x + \dfrac{\pi}{4}\right)$

2. $-15°$

3. $-\dfrac{4\pi}{3}, -\dfrac{2\pi}{3}, \dfrac{2\pi}{3}, \dfrac{4\pi}{3}$

4. $20°$

5. a. 2.5 **b.** $10; -7.5$ and $12.5; 10$

c. $\dfrac{15}{2\pi}; 15$ **d.** 25

CHAPTER 10 · Quiz 3

1. a. $\dfrac{\sqrt{3}}{3}$

b. -2

c. -1

2. Possible proof:

$\cos A \cot A + \sin A \overset{?}{=} \csc A$ — Original identity.

$\cos A\left(\dfrac{\cos A}{\sin A}\right) + \sin A \overset{?}{=} \csc A$ — Use the identity $\cot A = \dfrac{\cos A}{\sin A}$.

$\dfrac{\cos^2 A}{\sin A} + \sin A \overset{?}{=} \csc A$ — Multiply.

$\dfrac{\cos^2 A}{\sin A} + \dfrac{\sin^2 A}{\sin A} \overset{?}{=} \csc A$ — Rewrite $\sin A$ as $\dfrac{\sin^2 A}{\sin A}$.

$\dfrac{\sin^2 A + \cos^2 A}{\sin A} \overset{?}{=} \csc A$ — Add.

$\dfrac{1}{\sin A} \overset{?}{=} \csc A$ — Use the Pythagorean identity $\sin^2 A + \cos^2 A = 1$.

$\csc A = \csc A$ — Use the reciprocal identity $\csc A = \dfrac{1}{\sin A}$.

3. Possible proof:

$\sin\left(\dfrac{\pi}{2} + A\right) \overset{?}{=} \cos A$ — Original identity.

$\sin\dfrac{\pi}{2} \cdot \cos A + \cos\dfrac{\pi}{2} \cdot \sin A \overset{?}{=} \cos A$ — Use the sum identity for $\sin(A + B)$.

$1\cos A + 0\sin A \overset{?}{=} \cos A$ — $\cos\dfrac{\pi}{2} = 0$ and $\sin\dfrac{\pi}{2} = 1$.

$\cos A = \cos A$ — Multiply.

4. $\cos 60° = \dfrac{1}{2}$

5. $\dfrac{24}{25}$

CHAPTER 10 · Test

1. a. Quadrant IV; possible angle: $660°; \dfrac{5\pi}{3}$

b. Quadrant I; possible angle: $\dfrac{41\pi}{18}; 50°$

c. Quadrant II; possible angle: $525°; \dfrac{11\pi}{12}$

d. Quadrant III; possible angle: $\dfrac{9\pi}{8}; 157.5°$

2. a. $-\dfrac{\sqrt{2}}{2}$ **b.** $\dfrac{-\sqrt{3}}{2}$

c. $\dfrac{1}{2}$ **d.** $\dfrac{\sqrt{2} - \sqrt{6}}{4}$

3. a. Period: $\dfrac{\pi}{2}$; amplitude: 1; phase shift: π; vertical translation: -1

b.

c. Possible answer: $y = -1 + \sin 4\left(x + \dfrac{\pi}{8}\right)$

4. a. $\frac{15}{17}$ **b.** $-\frac{12}{5}$ **c.** $-\frac{\pi}{3}$

5. Domain of $x = \sin y$: $-1 \le x \le 1$; range of $x = \sin y$: all real numbers; domain of $y = \sin^{-1} x$: $-1 \le x \le 1$; range of $y = \sin^{-1} x$: $-\frac{\pi}{2} \le y \le \frac{\pi}{2}$

6. a. Possible answer: $y = -2 - \cos \frac{x}{2}$

b. Possible answer: $y = 2 \sin \pi x$

c. Possible answer: $y = 1 - \csc x$

7. $\frac{22\pi}{3}$ cm; 121π cm^2

8. a. Possible proof:

$\cot^2 A \overset{?}{=} \dfrac{1 + \cos 2A}{1 - \cos 2A}$ Original identity.

$\cot^2 A \overset{?}{=} \dfrac{1 + (\cos^2 A - \sin^2 A)}{1 - (\cos^2 A - \sin^2 A)}$ Use the double-angle identity for $\cos 2A$.

$\cot^2 A \overset{?}{=} \dfrac{(\sin^2 A + \cos^2 A) + (\cos^2 A - \sin^2 A)}{(\sin^2 A + \cos^2 A) - (\cos^2 A - \sin^2 A)}$ Use the Pythagorean identity $\sin^2 A + \cos^2 A = 1$.

$\cot^2 A \overset{?}{=} \dfrac{2 \cos^2 A}{2 \sin^2 A}$ Add.

$\cot^2 A \overset{?}{=} \left(\dfrac{\cos A}{\sin A}\right)^2$ $\frac{2}{2} = 1$ and $\frac{\cos^2 A}{\sin^2 A} = \left(\frac{\cos A}{\sin A}\right)^2$.

$\cot^2 A = \cot^2 A$ Use identity $\cot A = \frac{\cos A}{\sin A}$.

b. Possible proof:

$\tan\left(\dfrac{\pi}{2} - A\right) \overset{?}{=} \cot A$ Original identity.

$\dfrac{\sin\left(\dfrac{\pi}{2} - A\right)}{\cos\left(\dfrac{\pi}{2} - A\right)} \overset{?}{=} \cot A$ Use identity $\tan A = \frac{\sin A}{\cos A}$.

$\dfrac{\sin \frac{\pi}{2} \cos A - \cos \frac{\pi}{2} \sin A}{\cos \frac{\pi}{2} \cos A + \sin \frac{\pi}{2} \sin A} \overset{?}{=} \cot A$ Use identities for $\sin(A - B)$ and $\cos(A - B)$.

$\dfrac{1 \cdot \cos A - 0 \cdot \sin A}{0 \cdot \cos A + 1 \cdot \sin A} \overset{?}{=} \cot A$ $\sin \frac{\pi}{2} = 1$ and $\cos \frac{\pi}{2} = 0$.

$\dfrac{\cos A}{\sin A} \overset{?}{=} \cot A$ Multiply.

$\cot A = \cot A$ Use identity $\cot A = \frac{\cos A}{\sin A}$.

9. $\dfrac{\sqrt{2}}{2}$

10. 3.77, 6.23

SCORING RUBRICS

1. 5 Points

Answers are complete and correct. Explanations are clear, complete, and logical.

a. 3.08 m

b. 3.50 m. Possible explanation: First find distance d: $d = 4 \sin(0.385) \approx 1.50$. The maximum distance is $2d + 0.5$, or about 3.50 m.

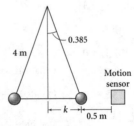

c. Use the formula to calculate the period, T:

$$T = 2\pi\sqrt{\dfrac{l}{g}} = 2\pi\sqrt{\dfrac{4}{9.8}} \approx 4.014$$

The period is about 4 s. The amplitude is about 1.50 m, half the distance between the maximum distance and the minimum distance.

d. Equation should be equivalent to $d = -1.50 \cos\left(\dfrac{\pi t}{2}\right) + 2$

e. About 3.43 m

f. About 0.7 s, 3.3 s, 4.7 s, and 7.3 s

3 Points

The answers to parts a–c are correct. In part d, one element of the equation (the horizontal scale factor, the vertical scale factor, the horizontal translation, or the vertical translation) is incorrect. The method used in part e is correct, but the answer is wrong because the equation is wrong. The answers to part f are incorrect or missing.

1 Point

The answers to parts a–c are correct, but the explanations may be unclear or incomplete. The answers to parts d–f are missing or incorrect.

2. 5 Points

Answers are correct and complete. Work and explanations are clear, complete, and logical.

a.

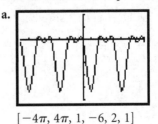

$[-4\pi, 4\pi, 1, -6, 2, 1]$

b. Yes; 2π

c. 3.3, 4.1, 5.3, 6.1

d. Possible answer: $y = -2\sin^2 x - 2\sin x - 0.3$

$y = 2\cos^2 x - 2\sin x - 2.3$	Original equation.
$y = 2(1 - \sin^2 x) - 2\sin x - 2.3$	Use the Pythagorean identity to substitute $1 - \sin^2 x$ for $\cos^2 x$.
$y = 2 - 2\sin^2 x - 2\sin x - 2.3$	Distribute the 2.
$y = -2\sin^2 x - 2\sin x - 0.3$	Add.

e. 6.098, 3.326, 5.328, 4.096

$-2\sin^2 x - 2\sin x - 0.3 = 0$	Original equation.
$\sin^2 x + \sin x + 0.15 = 0$	Divide by -2.
$\sin x = \dfrac{-1 \pm \sqrt{0.4}}{2}$	Use the quadratic formula.

$\sin^{-1}\left(\dfrac{-1 + \sqrt{0.4}}{2}\right) \approx -0.1848$, which is equivalent to $2\pi - 0.1848 \approx 6.098$. So one zero is 6.098.

Using the unit circle, another zero is $\pi + 0.1848$, or about 3.326.

$\sin^{-1}\left(\dfrac{-1 - \sqrt{0.4}}{2}\right) \approx -0.9549$, which is equivalent to $2\pi - 0.9549 \approx 5.328$. So one zero is 5.328.

Using the unit circle, another zero is $\pi + 0.9549$, or about 4.096.

3 Points
The answers to parts a, b, and d are complete and correct. Three of the four estimates in part c are correct. Part e is attempted, but the answers are incorrect.

1 Point
The answers to parts a and b are correct. Two of the estimates in part c are correct. The answers to parts d and e are missing or incorrect.

3. 5 Points
Answers are complete and correct. Methods may vary, but steps should be easy to follow.

a. $\sin 15° = \sin(45° - 30°)$

$= \sin 45° \cos 30° - \cos 45° \sin 30°$

$= \dfrac{\sqrt{2}}{2} \cdot \dfrac{\sqrt{3}}{2} - \dfrac{\sqrt{2}}{2} \cdot \dfrac{1}{2}$

$= \dfrac{\sqrt{6}}{4} - \dfrac{\sqrt{2}}{4}$

$= \dfrac{\sqrt{6} - \sqrt{2}}{4}$

b. $\cot 105° = \dfrac{\cos 105°}{\sin 105°}$

$= \dfrac{\cos(60° + 45°)}{\sin(60° + 45°)}$

$= \dfrac{\cos 60° \cos 45° - \sin 60° \sin 45°}{\sin 60° \cos 45° + \cos 60° \sin 45°}$

$= \dfrac{\dfrac{1}{2} \cdot \dfrac{\sqrt{2}}{2} - \dfrac{\sqrt{3}}{2} \cdot \dfrac{\sqrt{2}}{2}}{\dfrac{\sqrt{3}}{2} \cdot \dfrac{\sqrt{2}}{2} + \dfrac{1}{2} \cdot \dfrac{\sqrt{2}}{2}}$

$= \dfrac{\dfrac{\sqrt{2} - \sqrt{6}}{4}}{\dfrac{\sqrt{6} + \sqrt{2}}{4}}$

$= \dfrac{\sqrt{2} - \sqrt{6}}{\sqrt{6} + \sqrt{2}}$

$= \left(\dfrac{\sqrt{2} - \sqrt{6}}{\sqrt{6} + \sqrt{2}}\right)\left(\dfrac{\sqrt{6} - \sqrt{2}}{\sqrt{6} - \sqrt{2}}\right)$

$= \dfrac{2\sqrt{12} - 8}{4} = \dfrac{4\sqrt{3} - 8}{4} = \sqrt{3} - 2$

c. $\csc 255° = \dfrac{1}{\sin 255°}$

$= \dfrac{1}{-\sin 75°}$

$= \dfrac{1}{-\sin(45° + 30°)}$

$= \dfrac{1}{-\sin 45° \cos 30° - \cos 45° \sin 30°}$

$= \dfrac{1}{-\dfrac{\sqrt{2}}{2} \cdot \dfrac{\sqrt{3}}{2} - \dfrac{\sqrt{2}}{2} \cdot \dfrac{1}{2}}$

$= \dfrac{1}{\dfrac{-\sqrt{6} - \sqrt{2}}{4}}$

$= \dfrac{-4}{\sqrt{6} + \sqrt{2}}$

$= \left(\dfrac{-4}{\sqrt{6} + \sqrt{2}}\right)\left(\dfrac{\sqrt{6} - \sqrt{2}}{\sqrt{6} - \sqrt{2}}\right)$

$= -\sqrt{6} + \sqrt{2}$

3 Points
One of the following is true:

- Two of the answers are complete and correct. The third answer is attempted but is incorrect.

- All three answers are correct, but some steps are missing and/or the answers are not given in the correct form.

Discovering Advanced Algebra Assessment Resources B
©2004 Key Curriculum Press

1 Point

One of the following is true:

- One of the answers is correct, although it may not be expressed in the correct form. The other answers are missing or incorrect.

- All three answers are attempted, and at least some correct work is shown, but none of the answers are correct.

4. 5 Points

Answers are complete and correct. Explanations are clear, complete, and logical.

a. Equation should be equivalent to $y = 5t \sin \frac{\pi}{6} + 7$. Possible explanation: The center starts at a height of 7 ft. In t seconds, the center travels $5t$ ft along the cable, so the height increases by $5t \sin \frac{\pi}{6}$ ft. Therefore, the height, y, of the center above the ground after t seconds is $y = 5t \sin \frac{\pi}{6} + 7$.

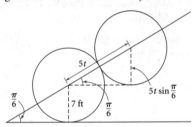

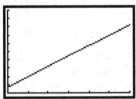

[0, 30, 5, 0, 100, 10]

b. Equation should be equivalent to $y = 7 \sin\left(-\frac{\pi}{5}\left(t - \frac{15}{2}\right)\right)$, or $y = -7 \cos \frac{\pi}{5} t$. Possible explanation: The wheel rotates 2π radians in 10 seconds, so it rotates $\frac{2\pi}{10}$, or $\frac{\pi}{5}$, radians in t seconds. In the diagram below, Sandra's height with respect to the center of the wheel after t seconds is the y-coordinate of her location S.

The angle θ in the diagram is the standard angle with the line from the center to S as its terminal side. So $y = 7 \sin \theta$. But $\theta = \frac{3\pi}{2} - \frac{\pi}{5} t$, so the equation is $y = 7 \sin\left(\frac{3\pi}{2} - \frac{\pi}{5} t\right)$, or $y = 7 \sin\left(-\frac{\pi}{5}\left(t - \frac{15}{2}\right)\right)$.

Using the identity for $\sin(A - B)$, the equation can be rewritten as $y = -7 \cos \frac{\pi}{5} t$.

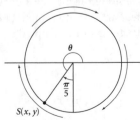

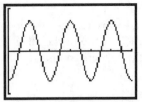

[0, 30, 5, −10, 10, 10]

c. Equation should be equivalent to $y = 5t \sin \frac{\pi}{6} + 7 - 7 \cos \frac{\pi}{5} t$. (This is the sum of the functions from parts a and b.)

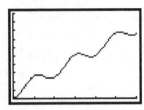

[0, 30, 5, 0, 100, 10]

d. 75 ft

e. About 26.0 s; 77.7 ft

f. Equations should be equivalent to $x = 5t \cos \frac{\pi}{6} + 7 \sin \frac{\pi}{5} t$ and $y = 5t \sin \frac{\pi}{6} + 7 - 7 \cos \frac{\pi}{5} t$.

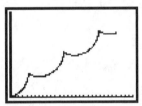

[0, 150, 5, 0, 100, 10]

$0 \le t \le 30$

Description should be clear and complete and should match the information shown in the graph. Possible description: The ride starts by accelerating up quickly. It then abruptly stops and drops slightly but then rises again, going faster and faster. This repeats once more. Shortly after the third time it drops in height, the ride is over just as one begins to rise again.

3 Points

One of the following is true:

- The answer to part a is correct. The answer to part b is not correct. The answers to parts c–e are consistent with the equation in part b but are incorrect because that equation is incorrect. In part f, the equation for x is incorrect, the equation for y is consistent with the equation in part c, and the description matches the (incorrect) graph.

- The answers to parts a–e are correct, but the explanations may be somewhat unclear. The answer to part f is missing or incorrect.

1 Point

The answer to part a is correct. The answer to part b is incorrect. At least two of the other parts are attempted, but the answers are incorrect.

CHAPTER 11 · Quiz 1

1. $-9 + 0 + 15 + 36$; 42   **2.** 4920   **3.** 2873

4. a. 198   **b.** 3348

CHAPTER 11 · Quiz 2

1. a. 40   **b.** About 120.59

  c. 39.921875   **d.** About 101.48

  e. 19.208

2. a. 3780 cm   **b.** 174,960 cm^2

CHAPTER 11 · Test

1. a. 551   **b.** u_{36} **c.** 4408   **d.** 2533

2. a. About 2.36   **b.** About 2490.56

  c. About 2412.04   **d.** 2500

3. $\sum_{n=1}^{\infty} 128\left(\dfrac{5}{8}\right)^{n-1} = 341\dfrac{1}{3}$

4. a. $30,678.10; $138,832.34

  b. $31,000; $140,000

  c. Yolanda; $160,137.77

5. a. 290   **b.** 56.25

  c. 950   **d.** About 308.31

  e. About 4558

6. a. 76   **b.** 4140

7. 448 cm

8. 14,280

CHAPTER 11 · Constructive Assessment Options

SCORING RUBRICS

1. 5 Points

Answers are correct and complete. Explanations are clear, logical, and supported by work.

a. Equation is a good fit. Possible answer: Consider 1991 to be year 1. Here is a plot of the data.

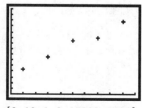

[0, 10, 1, 0, 15000, 1000]

The data are roughly linear, and the median-median line $\hat{y} = 990x + 3772$ appears to be a good fit.

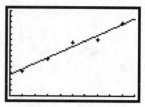

[0, 10, 1, 0, 15000, 1000]

b. Possible answer: The sum of the yearly expenditures for the last decade is approximately

$$\sum_{n=1}^{10}(990n + 3772) = \left(\dfrac{990}{2}\right)10^2 + \left(4762 - \dfrac{990}{2}\right)10$$

$$= 92170$$

So the estimated total sales are $92,170 million, or over $92 billion.

c. Possible answer: If the model is accurate, the total expenditure will be

$$\sum_{n=11}^{20}(990n + 3772) =$$

$$\left(\left(\dfrac{990}{2}\right)20^2 + \left(4762 - \dfrac{990}{2}\right)20\right) - 92170 =$$

$$191170$$

So the predicted total sales are $191,170 million, or over $191 billion. This may not be an accurate prediction. Technology changes, and CDs will probably be replaced by something new. For example, in the future, music may be sold primarily in the form of electronic files that are downloaded from the Internet. So although this model seems to fit the data for the 1990s quite well, it may not be a good predictor of sales in the current decade.

3 Points

The model in part a is a fairly good fit, and a reasonable explanation is provided. The predictions in parts b and c are correct based on the equation given in part a, but work and explanation may be incomplete or unclear. The explanation in part c is illogical or missing.

1 Point

The model in part a is a fairly good fit, and an explanation is given, although it may be somewhat unclear or incomplete. Part b is attempted, but the answer is incorrect. Part c is not attempted.

2. 5 Points

Answers are correct and complete. Explanations are clear, complete, and logical.

a. $\sum_{n=1}^{35} (2n - 1)$

b. 1225

c. 144; 64; 400

d. The sum of the first k odd numbers is k^2. The sum of the first 68 odd numbers is 68^2, or 4624.

e. 20,619. Possible explanation: 151 is the 76th odd number $(2(76) - 1 = 151)$, and 323 is the 162nd odd number $(2(162) - 1 = 323)$. So the sum of the odd numbers from 151 through 323 is $\sum_{n=76}^{162} (2n - 1) = \sum_{n=1}^{162} (2n - 1) - \sum_{n=1}^{75} (2n - 1)$, which is equal to $162^2 - 75^2$, or 20,619.

f. $\sum_{n=1}^{p} 2n$

g. $\sum_{n=1}^{p} 2n = p^2 + p$. Possible explanation: This is an arithmetic series with $u_1 = 2$ and $d = 2$, so $\sum_{n=1}^{p} 2n = \left(\frac{d}{2}\right)p^2 + \left(u_1 - \frac{d}{2}\right)p = \frac{2}{2}p^2 + \left(2 - \frac{2}{2}\right)p = p^2 + p$.

h. 702

i. 2142. Possible explanation: 82 is the 41st even number, and 122 is the 61st even number. So the sum of the even numbers from 82 through 122 is $\sum_{n=41}^{61} 2n = \sum_{n=1}^{61} 2n - \sum_{n=1}^{40} 2n$, which is equal to $\left(61^2 + 61\right) - \left(40^2 + 40\right)$, or 2142.

3 Points

At least eight parts of the nine parts are attempted. Six answers are correct, although the explanations, where required, may be somewhat unclear.

1 Point

At least four of the nine parts are attempted. Two of the answers are correct, although the explanations, where required, may be somewhat unclear.

3. 5 Points

Answers are complete and correct. Explanations are clear, complete, and logical.

a. i. About 62.3 cm². Students may add the area of each size square: $(6 \cdot 6) + 4(2 \cdot 2) + 16\left(\frac{2}{3} \cdot \frac{2}{3}\right) + 64\left(\frac{2}{9} \cdot \frac{2}{9}\right)$. Or they may recognize that the areas added at each stage form a geometric sequence with $u_0 = 36$ and $r = \frac{4}{9}$.

Thus, the area of Stage 3 is S_3 and can be calculated using the formula for the partial sum of a geometric series.

ii. About 64.7 cm². Students may use one of the methods discussed above.

iii. 64.8 cm². This can be found using the formula for the sum of a geometric series.

b. i. About 59.1 cm². Students may simply add the new areas added at each stage: $(6 \cdot 6) + 4(2 \cdot 2) + 12\left(\frac{2}{3} \cdot \frac{2}{3}\right) + 36\left(\frac{2}{9} \cdot \frac{2}{9}\right)$. Or they may recognize that the area of Stage 3 is $36 + S_2$, where S_2 is the third partial sum of the geometric series with $u_0 = 16$ and $r = \frac{1}{3}$.

ii. About 59.989 cm². Students may use one of the methods discussed above.

iii. 60 cm². This can be found by finding the sum of the geometric series described in part i and then adding 36.

c. The perimeter becomes infinitely large. Possible explanation: The perimeters of the first four stages are 24 cm, 40 cm, 56 cm, and 72 cm, respectively. The perimeters form an arithmetic series with $u_0 = 24$ and $d = 16$. The partial sums of the series get larger and larger. Therefore, the perimeter increases without bound.

3 Points

The answers to parts i and ii of both parts a and b are correct, and the accompanying work is clear and complete. The answer to part c is correct.

1 Point

Part i is correct in both parts a and b, and the accompanying work is clear and complete. The other answers are missing or incorrect.

4. 5 Points

Answers are complete and correct. Explanations are clear, complete, and logical.

a. Equations should be equivalent to:

Plan A: $S_n = 62.5n^2 + 62.5n$

Plan B: $S_n = 3000\left(1 - \left(\frac{2}{3}\right)^n\right)$

Possible explanation: The yearly payments under plan A form an arithmetic sequence with $u_1 = 125$ and $d = 125$. Therefore,

$$S_n = \left(\frac{d}{2}\right)n^2 + \left(u_1 - \frac{d}{2}\right)n$$

$$= \left(\frac{125}{2}\right)n^2 + \left(125 - \frac{125}{2}\right)n = 62.5n^2 + 62.5n$$

The yearly payments under plan B form a geometric sequence with $u_1 = 1000$ and $r = \frac{2}{3}$. Therefore,

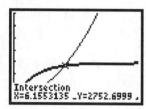

$$S_n = \frac{1000\left(1 - \left(\frac{2}{3}\right)^n\right)}{1 - \frac{2}{3}}$$

$$= 3000\left(1 - \left(\frac{2}{3}\right)^n\right)$$

b. Plan A is shown with the thinner line. The graphs intersect a little beyond $n = 6$. Before $n = 6$, the graph for plan A is below the graph for plan B, indicating that plan A is the better deal for the first six years. Beyond $n = 6$, the graph for plan B is below the graph for plan A, indicating that plan B is the better deal for year 7 and on.

```
Intersection
X=6.1553135  Y=2752.6999
```
[0, 15, 1, 0, 7000, 1000]

c. At least two factors should be described and supported. Possible answer: The Olsons need to think about how long they plan to be members. If they will be members for six or fewer years, plan A costs less. Otherwise, plan B is cheaper. They might also consider how much money they can afford to spend this year. Even if they plan to be members for more than six years, they may not have $1000 to spend this year. In that case, they may choose plan A even if it will ultimately be more expensive.

3 Points
The answer to parts a and b are complete and correct. Part c is attempted, but the answer is not reasonable.

1 Point
One of the following is true:

- Both equations are attempted in part a, but only one is correct. The answer to part b is based on the intersections of the graphs, but since one of the graphs is wrong, the answer is wrong. Part c is not attempted.

- Both equations in part a are correct. The answer to part b is incorrect. Part c is not attempted.

CHAPTER 12 • Quiz 1

1. a. .441   **b.** .208   **c.** .155

2. .5

3. a. About .082   **b.** About .066

4. .34

CHAPTER 12 • Quiz 2

1. a. $P(0 \text{ points}) = .2$; $P(1 \text{ point}) = .16$; $P(2 \text{ points}) = .64$

    b. 1.44 points

2. a. 13,000   **b.** About .0192

3. a. 120   **b.** About .167

CHAPTER 12 • Quiz 3

1. a. 220   **b.** 495

    c. 210   **d.** About .091

2. a^{14}; $3432a^7b^7$

3. $P(0 \text{ twos}) \approx .4823$; $P(1 \text{ two}) \approx .3858$; $P(2 \text{ twos}) \approx .1157$; $P(3 \text{ twos}) \approx .0154$; $P(4 \text{ twos}) \approx .0008$

CHAPTER 12 • Test

1. a. .196   **b.** 437

2. a. $\frac{1}{8}$, or .125   **b.** $\frac{7}{12}$, or about .5833

    c. 6

3. a. 1320   **b.** 364   **c.** 108

4. a. 512   **b.** $\frac{99}{4}z^5$ **c.** $190p^2q^{18}$

5. a. $\frac{1}{16}$, or .0625   **b.** $\frac{1}{17}$, or about .0588

    c. About .1055

6. .498

7. a. ii. $P(N \text{ and } I) = 0$

    iii. $P(N \text{ or } I) = .73$

    iv. $P(K \text{ and } I) = .06$

    v. $P(N \text{ and not } K) = .1$

    vi. $P(\text{not } K \text{ and not } N \text{ and not } I) = .15$

    b.

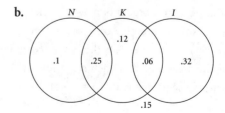

SCORING RUBRICS

1. 5 Points

Answers are correct, calculations are shown, and explanations are clear and correct.

a. i. $P(A \text{ or } B)$ is represented by the area covered by the two circles. The intersection of the two circles has two layers of coverage. In order not to count this overlapping area twice, the area of one of the layers must be subtracted from the sum of the areas of the two circles. Therefore, $P(A \text{ or } B) = P(A) + P(B) - P(A \text{ and } B)$.

ii. $P(A \text{ or } B) = .7 + .6 - (.7)(.6) = .88$;
$P(A \text{ or } C) = .7 + .5 - (.7)(.5) = .85$;
$P(C \text{ or } D) = .5 + .4 - (.5)(.4) = .7$

b.

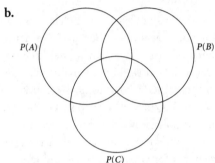

i. $P(A \text{ or } B \text{ or } C) = P(A) + P(B) + P(C) - P(A \text{ and } B) - P(A \text{ and } C) - P(B \text{ and } C) + P(A \text{ and } B \text{ and } C)$. Possible explanation: $P(A \text{ or } B \text{ or } C)$ is represented by the area covered by the three circles. Because the circles overlap (as pictured above), finding the sum of the areas of the circles, $P(A) + P(B) + P(C)$, counts the overlapping areas more than once. By subtracting the three regions representing $P(A \text{ and } B)$, $P(A \text{ and } C)$, and $P(B \text{ and } C)$, the three concave regions that were covered by two layers now have only one covering. But the middle region, representing $P(A \text{ and } B \text{ and } C)$, which was covered by three layers, now has no covering because the three regions subtracted overlap this region also. So $P(A \text{ and } B \text{ and } C)$ must be added back. So $P(A \text{ or } B \text{ or } C) = P(A) + P(B) + P(C) - P(A \text{ and } B) - P(A \text{ and } C) - P(B \text{ and } C) + P(A \text{ and } B \text{ and } C)$.

ii. $P(A \text{ or } B \text{ or } C) = .7 + .6 + .5 - (.7)(.6) - (.7)(.5) - (.6)(.5) + (.7)(.6)(.5) = .94$

$P(A \text{ or } C \text{ or } D) = .7 + .5 + .4 - (.7)(.5) - (.7)(.4) - (.5)(.4) + (.7)(.5)(.4) = .91$

$P(B \text{ or } C \text{ or } D) = .6 + .5 + .4 - (.6)(.5) - (.6)(.4) - (.5)(.4) + (.6)(.5)(.4) = .88$

c.

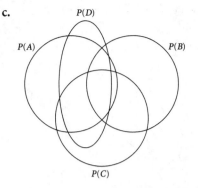

i. $P(A \text{ or } B \text{ or } C \text{ or } D) = P(A) + P(B) + P(C) + P(D) - P(A \text{ and } B) - P(A \text{ and } C) - P(A \text{ and } D) - P(B \text{ and } C) - P(B \text{ and } D) - P(C \text{ and } D) + P(A \text{ and } B \text{ and } C) + P(A \text{ and } B \text{ and } D) + P(A \text{ and } C \text{ and } D) + P(B \text{ and } C \text{ and } D) - P(A \text{ and } B \text{ and } C \text{ and } D)$

ii. $P(A \text{ or } B \text{ or } C \text{ or } D) = .7 + .6 + .5 + .4 - (.7)(.6) - (.7)(.5) - (.7)(.4) - (.6)(.5) - (.6)(.4) - (.5)(.4) + (.7)(.6)(.5) + (.7)(.6)(.4) + (.7)(.5)(.4) + (.6)(.5)(.4) - (.7)(.6)(.5)(.4) = .964$

d. i. $P(\text{not } A) = .3$; $P(\text{not } B) = .4$; $P(\text{not } C) = .5$; $P(\text{not } D) = .6$

ii. $P(\text{not } A \text{ and not } B \text{ and not } C \text{ and not } D) = (.3)(.4)(.5)(.6) = .036$

iii. $P(A \text{ or } B \text{ or } C \text{ or } D) = 1 - P(\text{not } A \text{ and not } B \text{ and not } C \text{ and not } D)$. This is because (not A and not B and not C and not D) is the complement of (A or B or C or D). In terms of a Venn diagram, $P(A \text{ or } B \text{ or } C \text{ or } D)$ is the area covered by the circles and $P(\text{not } A \text{ and not } B \text{ and not } C \text{ and not } D)$ is the area not covered. Together they make up all the possibilities. This is also a much faster way to calculate $P(A \text{ or } B \text{ or } C \text{ or } D)$.

3 Points

The answers to parts a and b are correct, but the explanations may be somewhat incomplete or unclear. Part ci is attempted, but one term of the answer is missing. The answer to part cii is consistent with the answer to part ci. The answers to parts di and dii are correct, but the answer to part dii is wrong because the answer to part cii is wrong.

1 Point

The answers to parts ai, bi, and di are correct. The other answers and explanations are missing or incorrect.

2. 5 Points

Answers are complete and correct. Explanations are clear, complete, and logical.

a. $1 \cdot \dfrac{48}{51} \cdot \dfrac{44}{50} \approx .828$

b. M represents "match" and N represents "no match."

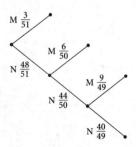

Turn 2nd Turn 3rd Turn 4th
card   card   card

 i. $P(\text{2-card win}) = \dfrac{3}{51} \approx .059$

 ii. $P(\text{3-card win}) = \dfrac{48}{51} \cdot \dfrac{6}{50} \approx .113$

 iii. $P(\text{4-card win}) = \dfrac{48}{51} \cdot \dfrac{44}{50} \cdot \dfrac{9}{49} \approx .152$

 iv. $P(\text{not winning with 4 cards}) = \dfrac{48}{51} \cdot \dfrac{44}{50} \cdot \dfrac{40}{49}$
   $\approx .676$

c. About 3.8 points. Possible explanation: The expected value—in this case, the expected score per game—is $10(.059) + 8(.113) + 6(.152) - 3(.676) = .378$. So in 10 games a player could expect to score $10(.378)$, or about 3.8 points.

d. 6 cards. Possible explanation: By extending the tree diagram, I found the least number for which the probability of losing was less than $\frac{1}{2}$.

$P(\text{losing with 5 cards}) = \dfrac{48}{51} \cdot \dfrac{44}{50} \cdot \dfrac{40}{49} \cdot \dfrac{36}{48}$
         $= .507$

$P(\text{losing with 6 cards}) = \dfrac{48}{51} \cdot \dfrac{44}{50} \cdot \dfrac{40}{49} \cdot \dfrac{36}{48} \cdot \dfrac{32}{47}$
         $= .345$

So the game has to be extended to 6 cards to make the probability of winning greater than the probability of losing.

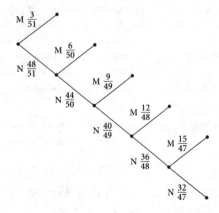

Turn 2nd Turn 3rd Turn 4th Turn 5th Turn 6th
card   card   card   card   card

---

3 Points
The answers to parts a and b are complete and correct. Either the answer to part c is correct or the answer to part d is correct.

1 Point
The answer to part a is correct. Three of the answers in part b are correct. The answers to parts c and d are missing or incorrect.

3. 5 Points
Answers are complete and correct. Explanations are clear, complete, and logical.

a. About $48\frac{1}{2}$ years. Possible explanation: There are 7!, or 5040 button sequences. If he uses two different sequences per week, he will use 104 in a year. So it will take $\frac{5040}{104}$, or about 48.5 years to go through them all.

b. About .055. Possible explanation: There are 11! ways the volunteers might be called. To figure out how many of these ways involve the three boys being called in a row, think of the boys as one unit and the other 8 volunteers as 8 individual units. Then there are 9! ways to order the 9 units. For each of these ways, there are 3! ways to order the three boys. So there are a total of (9!)(3!) arrangements for which the three boys are in order. Therefore, the probability that the three boys will be called in order is $\frac{(9!)(3!)}{11!}$, or about .055.

c. **i.** $_{12}C_9 = \dfrac{12!}{(3!)(9!)} = 220$

 ii. $_{12}P_9 = \dfrac{12!}{3!} = 79{,}833{,}600$

 iii. $\dfrac{_{10}C_7}{_{12}C_9} = \dfrac{120}{220} \approx .545$

 iv. $\dfrac{1}{12} \cdot \dfrac{3}{11} = \dfrac{3}{132} \approx .023$

3 Points
Four of the six answers are correct.

1 Points
Two of the six answers are correct.

4. 5 Points
Answers are complete and correct. Methods may vary.

a. $(.40)(.81) = .324$

b. $(.62)(.24) + (.72)(.18) + (.48)(.06) + (.81)(.40) + (.54)(.12) = .696$, or 69.6%

c. $\dfrac{0.324}{0.696}(73) \approx 34$

d. $(.4)(.19)(.12)(.54) \approx .005$

e. $(.62)(.72)(.48)(.81)(.54) \approx .094$

f. $_3C_2(0.62)^2(0.38)^1 + _3C_3(0.62)^3 \approx 0.677$

g. $_4C_0(0.46)^4 + {_4C_1}(0.54)^1(0.46)^3 +$
$_4C_2(0.54)^2(0.46)^2 \approx 0.625$

h. $1 - (.38)(.28)(.19) \approx .9798$

3 Points
Five of the eight answers are correct.

1 Point
Two of the eight answers are correct.

CHAPTER 13 · Quiz 1

1. a. 0   **b.** .875
   c. .5   **d.** Mode: 3; median: 4

2. $\mu = 50, \sigma = 10$

3. a. About 57%   **b.** About 31%

CHAPTER 13 · Quiz 2

1. a. -1.25 **b.** 128.96

2. (114.94, 119.06); (112.89, 121.11)

3. 4.8%

4. 2.5%

CHAPTER 13 · Quiz 3

1. a. $-.90$ **b.** .85   **c.** $-.56$ **d.** .09

2. a. $\hat{y} = 2.5528x + 89.04$

   b. 3.5711

   c. 91.6 thousand; the prediction is 3.2 thousand (or 3.4%) less than the actual value.

3. a. $\hat{y} = 1.43x^2 - 2.31x + 2.6$;
$\hat{y} = 0.22x^3 - 0.90x^2 + 4.73x - 3$

   b. 1.316; 1.340

CHAPTER 13 · Test

1. a. 3   **b.** .6   **c.** .4   **d.** 0

2. a. The distribution is approximately normal.

   b. $\bar{x} \approx 97.5$; $s \approx 1.98$

3. a. The data appear to be linear. The correlation coefficient, .96, is very close to 1, indicating a strong linear relationship.

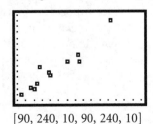

[90, 240, 10, 90, 240, 10]

b. $\hat{y} = 1.08x - 2.21$. The slope is the increase in the 2000 median home price per increase of $1000 in the 1999 median home price. The y-intercept is the 2000 median home price for a city whose 1999 median home price was $0. This value doesn't make much sense in the real world because the median home price would not be $0 or a negative value.

   c. 10.38

   d. $143,900

4. a. About 15.7%   **b.** About 28.7%
   c. About 2.1%   **d.** About 0.30%

5. No; if the mean were 30 minutes, then there would be only a 1.9% chance that a 25-trip sample would have a mean of 35 minutes or more.

6. Between 44.17 mi/gal and 47.83 mi/gal

7. a. $\hat{y} = -35.97x^2 + 1145.62x + 2019.26$

   b. $\hat{y} = -1.62x^3 + 19.92x^2 + 581.04x + 3584.19$

   c. The first graph shows the quadratic model. The second graph shows the cubic model. The cubic model appears to be a better fit.

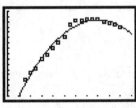

[0, 22, 2, 4000, 12000, 500]

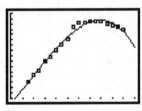

[0, 22, 2, 4000, 12000, 500]

   d. Quadratic model: 301.15; cubic model: 237.40. The cubic model is a better fit.

   e. 9568

   f. 2007

CHAPTER 13 · Constructive Assessment Options

SCORING RUBRICS

1. 5 Points
Answers are complete and correct. Explanations are clear, complete, and logical.

   a. .9988

   b. .9892

c. Both correlation coefficients are close to 1, indicating strong linear relationships. The linear relationship between year and food and beverage CPI is slightly stronger than the linear relationship between year and medical care cost.

d. $r(year, \log(medical\ CPI)) \approx .9938$; $r(\log(year), \log(medical\ CPI)) \approx .9920$

e. $\log y = 0.0300x + 1.2589$

$$y = 10^{0.0300x+1.2589}$$
$$y = \left(10^{0.0300x}\right)\left(10^{1.2589}\right)$$
$$y = 18.15\left(10^{0.0300}\right)^{x}$$
$$\hat{y} = 18.15(1.072)^{x}$$

f. $s = 18.11$

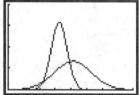

[0, 50, 10, 0, 275, 25]

3 Points

The answers to parts a–d are complete and correct. The equation in part e is incorrect, so the graph and root mean square error in part f are incorrect.

1 Point

The answers to parts a and b are correct. Part c is attempted, but the comments are incorrect or irrelevant. The answers to parts d–f are missing or incorrect.

2. 5 Points

Answers are correct. Explanations are clear and complete.

a.

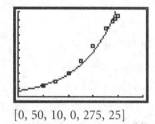

[0, 40, 4, 0, .2, .05]

Answer should be consistent with the graphs. Possible answer: The route to school may be downhill, resulting in a shorter mean time. Alison may leave home a little later than she should in the morning and have to ride quickly to get to school on time. There is little variation in the home-to-school times, perhaps because Alison is just focused on getting to school. On the way home from school, Alison may be tired or may just want to take a more leisurely ride. She may stop to chat with her friends. But she does get home quickly sometimes.

b. $0.7; -0.\overline{4}$

c. 24%; 67%

d. 6% of the time, or about once every 16 days

e. 24% of the time, or about once every four trips. Possible explanation: She makes the trip to school in less than 15 minutes about 31% of the time. She makes the trip home from school in less than 15 minutes 17% of the time. Because the number of trips to school is the same as the number from school, the overall percentage is the average of 31% and 17%, or 24%. Thus, about 24% of the time, or about once in every four trips, she makes a trip in less than 15 minutes.

f. She makes her very fastest trips coming home more often than going to school. If you look at the extreme left of the screen showing the two graphs, you can see that the school-to-home curve is above the home-to-school curve. These are relative frequency curves, but because the total number of trips going and coming is the same, the higher curve indicates the greater number of trips for that time.

3 Points

The answers to parts a–d are correct. Part e is attempted, but the answer is incorrect or no explanation is given. The answer to part f is missing or incorrect.

1 Point

Two of the answers from parts a–d are correct. The answers to parts e and f are missing or incorrect.

3. 5 Points

Answers are complete and correct.

a. Domestic animals: $\bar{x}_{GP} = 117$, $s_{GP} \approx 102.2$; $\bar{x}_L = 75$, $s_L \approx 5.3$; wild animals: $\bar{x}_{GP} = 219.6$, $s_{GP} \approx 228.1$; $\bar{x}_L = 13.6$, $s_L \approx 10.3$

b. Domestic animals: $r \approx .83$; wild animals: $r \approx .92$

c. Domestic animals: $\hat{y} = 0.043x + 5.65$; $s \approx 3.2$; wild animals: $\hat{y} = 0.042x + 4.39$; $s \approx 4.3$

d. Domestic animals: $\hat{y} = 0.038x + 6.96$; $s \approx 3.4$; wild animals: $\hat{y} = 0.039x + 6.12$; $s \approx 4.6$

e. Possible answer: The correlation coefficient for wild animals, .92, is better than the coefficient for domestic animals, which is .83. However, in both cases, the root mean square error for domestic animals is smaller than for wild animals, so I would probably be more confident of my predictions for domestic animals. In both cases, the least squares line has a smaller root mean square error than the median-median line, so I would use those models.

3 Points

Twelve or 13 of the 18 answers in parts a–d are correct.

1 Point

Seven or 8 of the 18 answers in parts a–d are correct.

CHAPTERS 10–13 · Exam

1. a. $-\dfrac{1}{2}$ **b.** $\sqrt{2}$

    c. $-\dfrac{\sqrt{3}}{3}$ **d.** $\dfrac{\sqrt{6}-\sqrt{2}}{4}$

    e. $-\dfrac{8}{15}$ **f.** $65°$

2. 64; 544

3. $\dfrac{15\pi}{4}$ in.; $\dfrac{135\pi}{8}$ in.^{2}

4. a. 1028.5   **b.** 343.75   **c.** 131,175.981

5. The company's claim does not appear to be accurate. The mean for this sample is 61.53, and the standard deviation is 3.26. If the company's claim is accurate, then the probability of getting a mean of 61.53 or greater is only $N\left(61.53, 100, 60, \dfrac{3.26}{\sqrt{30}}\right) \approx$ .0051, or about 0.51%.

6. a. .175   **b.** .775   **c.** .6

7. a. Possible answer: $y = -\cos 2\pi x + 2$

    b. Possible answer: $y = -1 + \cos 2x$

8. a. 1,679,616   **b.** 175,760

    c. 703,040   **d.** About .25; about .003

9. a. $P(0 \text{ bull's-eyes}) = .0023$, $P(1 \text{ bull's-eye}) = .0332$, $P(2 \text{ bull's-eyes}) = .1767$, $P(3 \text{ bull's-eyes}) = .4176$, $P(4 \text{ bull's-eyes}) = .3702$

    b. About 31.2 points

10. a. .9957   **b.** $\hat{y} = 0.918x + 1.057$

    c. $\hat{y} = 1.753x^{0.736}$ **d.** $\hat{y} = 1.756(1.251)^x$

    e. Least squares line: 0.168; power model: 0.155; exponential model: .640. The power model, $y = 1.753x^{0.736}$, is the best fit.

Final Exam

1. a. $u_1 = 15625$ and $u_n = 0.6u_{n-1}$ where $n \geq 2$

    b. $u_n = 15625(0.6)^{n-1}$

    c. $u_{10} = 157.484$

    d. $S_{10} = 38826.304$

    e. $S = 39062.5$

2.

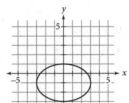
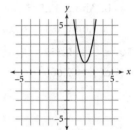

    a. .32256   **b.** .03136

    c. .45952   **d.** .78208

3. a.   **b.**

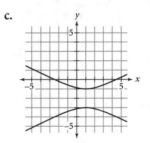

    c.

4. a. Vertices: $(-3, -1)$ and $(3, -1)$; foci: $\left(\sqrt{5}, -1\right)$ and $\left(-\sqrt{5}, -1\right)$

    b. Vertex: $(2, 1)$; focus: $(2, 1.75)$; directrix: $y = 0.25$

    c. Vertices: $(1, -1)$ and $(1, -3)$; foci: $\left(1, -2 + \sqrt{3}\right)$ and $\left(1, -2 - \sqrt{3}\right)$

5. $f(x) = (x + 3i)(x - 3i)(x - 2)\left(x - \dfrac{1}{2}\right)$

6. a. $mean \approx 3.529$; $median = 4$; $mode = 4$

    b.

    Five-number summary: 1, 2, 4, 5, 6. The data are skewed left, so more data values fall above the mean than below it.

    c. $s \approx 1.663$

    d. Between 1.867 and 5.192 kittens, or between 2 and 5 kittens

7. a. $x = 11t$, $y = -4.9t^2$, or $x = 11t$, $y = -4.9t^2 + 130$

    b. 56.661 m from the base of the cliff; 5.151 s

8. a.
$$\begin{bmatrix} 1 & 1 & -1 \\ 2 & 2 & -3 \\ 2 & 1 & 1 \end{bmatrix} \begin{bmatrix} a \\ b \\ c \end{bmatrix} = \begin{bmatrix} -10 \\ -23 \\ -2 \end{bmatrix} \text{ or}$$

$$\begin{bmatrix} 1 & 1 & -1 & -10 \\ 2 & 2 & -3 & -23 \\ 2 & 1 & 1 & -2 \end{bmatrix}$$

b. $a = 2$, $b = -9$, $c = 3$. Answers may include solving by multiplying an answer matrix by the inverse of the coefficient matrix, by writing an augmented matrix and finding the reduced row-echelon form, or by using the elimination method.

9. a. $y = 15 + 3 \cos 14\pi x$

b. About 12.573 cm

c. About 0.043 s, 0.099 s, 0.186 s, and 0.242 s

10. a. $x \approx 0.352$ **b.** $x \approx 4.667$

c. $x \approx 2.605$ **d.** $x \approx 1.432$

11. a. $\hat{y} = 0.0083x - 0.4860$

b. 0.0315; the sum of the residuals is small, so the line is a good fit.

c. The slope 0.0083 means that the cost of mailing a letter increased by about 0.83 cent (or 0.0093 dollar) each year, and the y-intercept -0.486 means that the cost was -48 cents in 1900, which doesn't make sense, so the y-intercept has no real-world meaning.

12. a. $y = 1.2(x + 2.2)(x - 4.6)$

b. $y = 1.2x^2 - 2.88x - 12.144$

c. $y = 1.2(x - 1.2)^2 - 13.872$

13. $r \approx .845$; there is a fair positive linear association between the two variables.

14. a. 98,770

b. 592,620

Discovering Advanced Algebra Assessment Resources B
©2004 Key Curriculum Press